Clear**Revise**®

AQA GCSE
English Literature

Illustrated revision and practice

A Christmas Carol
By Charles Dickens

Published by
PG Online Limited
The Old Coach House
35 Main Road
Tolpuddle
Dorset
DT2 7EW
United Kingdom

sales@pgonline.co.uk
www.clearrevise.com
www.pgonline.co.uk
2023

PG ONLINE

PREFACE

Absolute clarity! That's the aim.

This is everything you need to ace the question on *A Christmas Carol* and beam with pride. The content is laid out in a beautifully illustrated format that is clear, approachable and as concise and simple as possible.

The checklist on the contents pages will help you keep track of what you have already worked through and what's left before the big day.

We have included worked exam-style questions with answers. There is also an exam-style question at the end of the book. You can check your answer against that given on page 62.

LEVELS OF LEARNING

Based on the degree to which you are able to truly understand a new topic, we recommend that you work in stages. Start by reading a short explanation of something, then try to recall what you've just read. This will have limited effect if you stop there but it aids the next stage. Question everything. Write down your own summary and then complete and mark a related exam-style question. Cover up the answers if necessary but learn from them once you've seen them. Lastly, teach someone else. Explain the topic in a way that they can understand. Have a go at the different practice questions – they offer an insight into how and where marks are awarded.

Design and artwork: Jessica Webb & Mike Bloys / PG Online Ltd

First edition 2023   10 9 8 7 6 5 4 3 2 1
A catalogue entry for this book is available from the British Library
ISBN: 978-1-910523-49-0
Copyright © PG Online 2023
All rights reserved

Printed on FSC certified paper by Bell and Bain Ltd, Glasgow, UK.

THE SCIENCE OF REVISION

Illustrations and words

Research has shown that revising with words and pictures doubles the quality of responses by students.[1] This is known as 'dual-coding' because it provides two ways of fetching the information from our brain. The improvement in responses is particularly apparent in students when they are asked to apply their knowledge to different problems. Recall, application and judgement are all specifically and carefully assessed in public examination questions.

Retrieval of information

Retrieval practice encourages students to come up with answers to questions.[2] The closer the question is to one you might see in a real examination, the better. Also, the closer the environment in which a student revises is to the 'examination environment', the better. Students who had a test 2–7 days away did 30% better using retrieval practice than students who simply read, or repeatedly reread material. Students who were expected to teach the content to someone else after their revision period did better still.[3] What was found to be most interesting in other studies is that students using retrieval methods and testing for revision were also more resilient to the introduction of stress.[4]

Ebbinghaus' forgetting curve and spaced learning

Ebbinghaus' 140-year-old study examined the rate at which we forget things over time. The findings still hold true. However, the act of forgetting facts and techniques and relearning them is what cements them into the brain.[5] Spacing out revision is more effective than cramming – we know that, but students should also know that the space between revisiting material should vary depending on how far away the examination is. A cyclical approach is required. An examination 12 months away necessitates revisiting covered material about once a month. A test in 30 days should have topics revisited every 3 days – intervals of roughly a tenth of the time available.[6]

Summary

Students: the more tests and past questions you do, in an environment as close to examination conditions as possible, the better you are likely to perform on the day. If you prefer to listen to music while you revise, tunes without lyrics will be far less detrimental to your memory and retention. Silence is most effective.[5] If you choose to study with friends, choose carefully – effort is contagious.[7]

1. Mayer, R. E., & Anderson, R. B. (1991). Animations need narrations: An experimental test of dual-coding hypothesis. *Journal of Education Psychology*, (83)4, 484–490.

2. Roediger III, H. L., & Karpicke, J.D. (2006). Test-enhanced learning: Taking memory tests improves long-term retention. *Psychological Science*, 17(3), 249–255.

3. Nestojko, J., Bui, D., Kornell, N. & Bjork, E. (2014). Expecting to teach enhances learning and organisation of knowledge in free recall of text passages. *Memory and Cognition*, 42(7), 1038–1048.

4. Smith, A. M., Floerke, V. A., & Thomas, A. K. (2016) Retrieval practice protects memory against acute stress. *Science*, 354(6315), 1046–1048.

5. Perham, N., & Currie, H. (2014). Does listening to preferred music improve comprehension performance? *Applied Cognitive Psychology*, 28(2), 279–284.

6. Cepeda, N. J., Vul, E., Rohrer, D., Wixted, J. T. & Pashler, H. (2008). Spacing effects in learning a temporal ridgeline of optimal retention. *Psychological Science*, 19(11), 1095–1102.

7. Busch, B. & Watson, E. (2019), *The Science of Learning*, 1st ed. Routledge.

CONTENTS

MARK ALLOCATIONS

All the questions in this book require extended responses. These answers should be marked as a whole in accordance with the levels of response guidance on **page 61**. The answers provided are examples only. There are many more points to make than there are marks available, so the answers are not exhaustive.

ASSESSMENT OBJECTIVES

In the exam, your answers will be marked against assessment objectives (AOs). It's important you understand which skills each AO tests.

AO1

- Show the ability to read, understand and respond to texts.
- Answers should maintain a critical style and develop an informed personal response.
- Use examples from the text, including quotes, to support and illustrate points.

AO2

- Analyse the language, form and structure used by a writer to create meanings and effects, using relevant subject terminology where appropriate.

AO3

- Show understanding of the relationships between texts and the contexts in which they were written.

AO4

- Use a range of vocabulary and sentence structures for clarity, purpose and effect, with accurate spelling and punctuation.

The AOs on this page have been written in simple language. See the AQA website for the official wording.

PAPER 1
Shakespeare and the 19th-century novel

Information about Paper 1

Written exam: 1 hours 45 minutes (this includes the questions on Shakespeare)

64 marks (30 marks for Shakespeare plus 4 marks for SPaG, and 30 marks for the 19th-century novel)

40% of the qualification grade (20% each for Shakespeare and the 19th-century novel)

This guide covers the section on the 19th-century novel.

Questions
One extended-writing question per text

DICKENS AND *A CHRISTMAS CAROL*

A Christmas Carol is a story by Charles Dickens which was first published in 1843.

Charles Dickens

Charles Dickens (1812–1870) is one of the best-known British writers. He wrote over a dozen novels, including *Oliver Twist*, *Great Expectations*, *Little Dorrit* and *A Tale of Two Cities*.

He had a relatively comfortable childhood, but in 1824, his father was imprisoned for unpaid debts when Charles was 12. Charles' mother joined her husband in debtors' prison (which was usual at the time). While his parents were in prison, Charles left school and worked at a boot blacking factory to support himself, working ten-hour days.

Comment: Dickens' experiences of the prison system and child labour influenced his attitudes towards social reform.

Many of Dickens' novels, including *A Christmas Carol*, reference social injustice, poverty and crime, and Dickens was critical of how the poor were treated by society. The popularity of Dickens' novels meant his message about social reform reached a large audience, and his readers recognised that more needed to be done to help the less fortunate. Turn to **pages 5–8** for more on Victorian social problems and social reform.

Charles Dickens

A Christmas Carol

A Christmas Carol has elements of the **ghost story** genre and is an example of a **morality tale**.

Ghost stories: The story's full title is: *A Christmas Carol. In Prose. Being a Ghost Story of Christmas*.

"Prose" just means 'written without rhythm'. This clarifies to the reader that it isn't a book of Christmas songs

A Christmas Carol features several supernatural elements:

Ghosts: Scrooge is visited by four different ghosts.

Time travel: Scrooge travels backwards and forwards through time.

Location hops: The ghosts magically transport Scrooge across London, as well as to his childhood village, a moor, a lighthouse and on to a ship.

Stories with supernatural elements were popular in the 19th century because they offered readers an escape from everyday life.

Morality tale: *A Christmas Carol* is a **morality tale**. Morality tales are stories that try to teach the reader a lesson and encourage them to change for the better. In *A Christmas Carol*, Dickens wanted readers to understand the importance of compassion towards others, especially those who were living in poverty (see **page 6** for more on poverty in the Victorian era) and to make society fairer for everyone. Dickens uses the character of Scrooge to show that even the most selfish people can change for the better (see **pages 47–49** for more on the theme of redemption).

Comment: Although the novella has a moral, Dickens didn't want the story to come across as preachy; he also wanted to make sure his readers were entertained. Dickens does this by trying to evoke a variety of emotions from his readers with elements that are exciting, scary, heart-warming, and humorous.

Popularity of *A Christmas Carol*

Dickens' writing was very popular amongst Victorians. His novels appealed to most people in society, but especially to the working class. Many of his characters were poor, and faced hardships that his poorer readers would have recognised.

Comment: Working-class readers would have empathised with the struggles and difficulties faced by the Cratchit family.

Dickens initially printed 6,000 copies of *A Christmas Carol*, and it quickly sold out. Since its publication, *A Christmas Carol* has never been out of print, showing its universal popularity.

Most working-class Victorians were illiterate, so if they wanted to read a book, they had to find someone who could read it aloud to them. The title of *A Christmas Carol* could allude to the idea that the novella was meant to be listened to, just like a Christmas carol.

The introduction page to *A Christmas Carol*

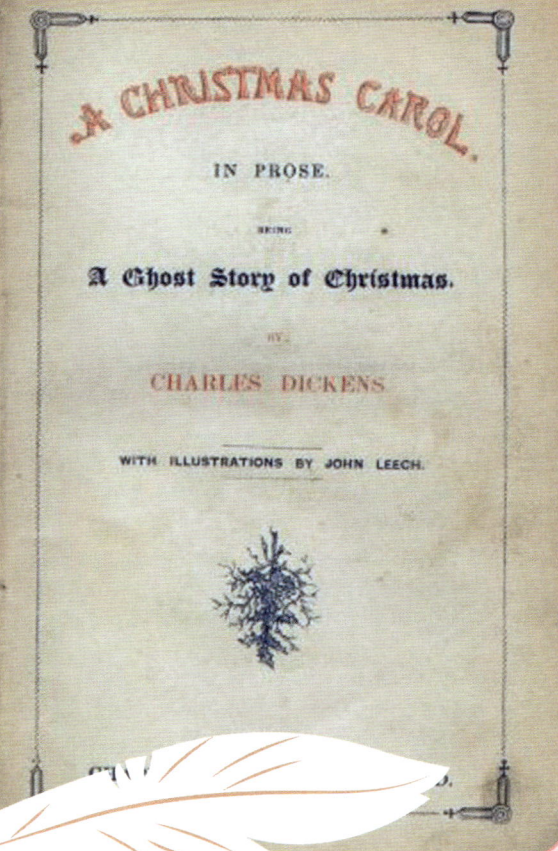

CONTEXT

The context of the Victorian period is important for understanding the deeper meaning of the novella.

 You need to comment on context to get marks for AO3 (**page vi**).

Setting

The year the story takes place is never confirmed, but it is likely to be around the time the novella was written (1843), and most of the events take place in London.

Comment: Setting the story in London allowed Dickens to highlight the inequality between the rich and poor more easily. Since the two groups lived in close proximity of each other, this made the issue of poverty more pronounced.

The years between 1837–1901 are known as the Victorian period, because this is when Queen Victoria was on the throne.

The events of the novella unfold over three days: Christmas Eve, Christmas Day and Boxing Day.

Comment: Dickens chose to set his novella over the Christmas period because it is a holiday associated with kindness and forgiveness, two important themes in the story. Dickens wanted his readers to act with kindness and forgiveness all year round. For more on the theme of Christmas spirit, turn to **pages 52–53**.

Class

British society in the 19th century could be categorised into three classes: upper, middle and working class. The class system was fixed, and it was difficult to move up the hierarchy. Upper-class families were the richest members of society and belonged to the aristocracy (families with inherited land and wealth). Upper-class families probably made up about 5% of the population. Those in the middle-class, like Scrooge, had money, but they earned it through running their own businesses. They accounted for approximately 15% of the population.

Comment: Scrooge owns a *"counting-house"*. This is similar to a modern accountancy firm where accountants record financial transactions made by businesses. It's also implied that Scrooge is a money lender who profits from loaning money to the poor. In Stave Four, the Ghost of Christmas Yet to Come shows a family who owe money to Scrooge.

Class continued

The remainder of society (approximately 80% of the population) belonged to the working class. Working class families were often poor, and needed to work for a living, often in tough, unskilled jobs. Employees didn't have any workplace rights, and the pay was often low. Workers were prepared to put up with bad conditions and poor treatment because they didn't want to lose their jobs.

Comment: Scrooge treats Bob Cratchit very poorly. Bob is underpaid and is expected to work in freezing conditions. Bob doesn't complain because he is fearful of losing his job and his means of supporting his family.

In working-class families, everyone who was old enough to work was expected to have a job to contribute to the family's income, this included children as young as four.

Comment: Martha, Bob Cratchit's daughter, is a *"poor apprentice at a milliner's"* (hat maker). She's late for the family Christmas because she was working on Christmas morning.

A Victorian chimney sweep

Business owners often preferred to employ children as their wages were cheaper than an adult's, and their small size meant they could do jobs that adults couldn't, such as climbing inside chimneys to sweep them or crawling under machinery. Children often worked very long hours for very little pay, and the work could be dangerous, for example, chimney sweeps could get stuck up chimneys, and factory workers could lose fingers or limbs in accidents at work. Most poor children didn't go to school because they needed to work instead. This meant that poor people were trapped in a cycle of poverty: because they didn't have an education, they weren't qualified for better paying jobs.

Comment: Dickens uses the character of Ignorance to highlight this problem. See **page 46**.

In 1842 and 1843, reports were published about child labour in mines and factories. The findings in the reports led to calls for better workplace safety for children.

Comment: Dickens read these reports and was shocked and appalled. He initially wanted to write a pamphlet against child labour, but instead he decided to write *A Christmas Carol* to make more people aware of social problems.

Some Victorians were prejudiced towards the working class. They thought people were poor because they were lazy. Those with money didn't understand how difficult it was to escape poverty.

Comment: In Stave One, Scrooge demonstrates this prejudice. He refuses to donate money to the charity collectors because he *"can't afford to make idle people merry"*.

Poverty

Poverty was a widespread problem in Victorian England, especially in cities.

The Industrial Revolution

From the mid-1700s, Britain experienced the **Industrial Revolution**. British manufacturing began to move away from hand production and instead used steam-powered machines in factories. Often these factories were built in cities, so people looking for work migrated to urban areas in search of jobs. This caused an enormous influx of people moving to cities, especially London, which created social issues.

The Industrial Revolution made a lot of business people extremely wealthy, while the factory workers experienced poverty. This widened the divide between the rich and poor.

Housing

The migration of people to urban areas created demand for affordable housing. Many people could only afford to live in **slums** (areas of housing which offered cheap accommodation) but slums were often overcrowded and unsanitary. This meant that disease spread quickly.

A drawing of a slum from 1840. Children play in a pile of rubbish while a woman searches through the pile for food scraps.

Comment: Bob Cratchit, his wife and their six children live in a *"four-roomed house"*, whereas Scrooge has several rooms all to himself. He even has a *"lumber-room"*: a room used for storing unused furniture. This highlights how the richer members of society had more space than they need, whereas the poor are cramped into spaces which were too small.

Nutrition

Poor harvests resulted in a shortage of affordable food in England during the 19th century, and many working-class people were malnourished. This contributed to ill health and lower life expectancy in the period.

Comment: The charity collectors are described as *"portly"*. This indicates their wealth, as only the very rich had enough food to make them overweight.

Victorian solutions to crime and poverty

In the 1800s, the government didn't offer much help for those in poverty. Unlike today, there was no National Health Service (NHS) or monetary benefits for people who were struggling.

Comment: Scrooge refuses to donate to charity because his taxes contribute to *"workhouses"*, *"prisons"* and *"the Treadmill"*. Scrooge thinks that enough is already done to deal with poverty.

The workhouse

Workhouses were institutions where the very poor could get food and shelter in exchange for work. However, life in the workhouse was deliberately difficult to deter only the most desperate from staying. Workhouse routines were strict and repetitive with little food and poor conditions. Men and women were kept apart, so husbands and wives, and brothers and sisters were split up, with little chance of seeing each other. Male inmates could be expected to do tough manual labour, such as breaking rocks or turning a mill. Female inmates could spend long hours washing laundry.

An impoverished couple say goodbye before they are separated in the workhouse.

Prisons

Like workhouses, **prisons** were designed to be unpleasant places to deter inmates from re-offending once they had been released. Prisons were often overcrowded and dirty, and prison staff focused on punishment (such as the treadmill, below) rather than rehabilitation. People could be sent to prison for very minor offences, such as public drunkenness or petty theft.

Comment: Dickens' own experiences of his family being in jail (see **page 2**) influenced his negative attitudes towards the prison system.

The treadmill

The **treadmill** was a form of manual labour used in prisons as punishment. It was a large, human-powered wheel, where inmates would step on a wheel to turn it, and the wheel would grind corn or generate power for pumps. Prisoners could walk on the treadmill for six hours a day.

Prisoners turn a treadmill by stepping on the wheel.

Victorian attitudes to poverty

The Poor Law

Prior to 1843, middle- and upper-class people paid taxes which contributed to relief for the poor. Some taxpayers felt that the poor were lazy, and didn't deserve taxpayer money. In 1843, a few months before *A Christmas Carol* was published, a new **Poor Law** was introduced which aimed to reduce the amount of taxes paid by the wealthy. This new Poor Law decreed that more workhouses should be built, and poor people should only be allowed access to help if they were prepared to go to the workhouse.

Comment: The charity collectors say that *"many would rather die"* than go to the workhouse. Some social reformers, such as Dickens, believed that increasing the capacity of workhouses was not the answer to the problem of poverty.

Dickens believed that if the working classes were paid a fairer wage, there would be less need for poor relief as families would be able to support themselves.

Comment: At the end of *A Christmas Carol*, Scrooge recognises the importance of looking after the working class and he gives Bob Cratchit a pay rise. Dickens wanted to encourage employers to treat their staff fairly.

Thomas Malthus

Thomas Malthus (1766–1834) was an English economist. He believed that poverty was inevitable because population growth would always outpace food production. He thought this would lead to many poor people dying from starvation, but he saw these deaths as unavoidable.

Comment: Scrooge comments of the poor: *"If they would rather die... they had better do it, and decrease the surplus population"*. Like Malthus, Scrooge sees the poor as disposable.

Dickens did not agree with Malthus. He believed that there was enough food, it just needed to be more affordable and shared more fairly.

Comment: In Stave Three, Dickens describes an array of food for sale, including chestnuts, onions, pears, apples, raisins, almonds, figs and plums. Dickens suggests that there was plenty of food to go around.

FEATURES OF THE NOVELLA

A Christmas Carol is a novella: a short novel.

Staves

The novella has five chapters which Dickens calls 'staves'. Staves are also the five lines that musical notes are written on, so this links to the musical title of *A Christmas Carol*.

 The exam paper might refer to 'Chapters' instead of 'Staves'. Don't worry, they mean the same thing.

Narrator

A Christmas Carol uses an unnamed, **first-person narrator** to tell parts of the story. The reader never discovers the narrator's identity, but it's implied it is someone who is familiar with Scrooge, as he knows a lot about Scrooge's personality. The narrator conveys his disapproval of Scrooge, describing him as a *"covetous, old sinner"*, which encourages the reader to dislike Scrooge too.

The narrator often uses a **conversational tone**, as well as imaginative and humorous descriptions, to make the story more entertaining for the reader: *"I might have been inclined, myself, to regard a coffin-nail as the deadest piece of ironmongery in the trade"*.

Comment: Telling parts of the story from a first-person perspective, as well as using a familiar tone, helps create a closer relationship between the narrator and the reader. It also makes the novella seem more believable, as if the narrator is recalling actual events.

Structure

Much of the novella is set in Scrooge's present, with the action unfolding between Christmas Eve and Boxing Day. However, there are **time hops** when the ghosts visit Scrooge and show him the past, present and future. This allows the reader to witness how Scrooge's past has shaped him, and the events which lead to his redemption.

Comment: Each of the ghosts only have a short amount of time with Scrooge. This increases the pace and urgency of the story: Scrooge must learn his lesson before time runs out.

LANGUAGE TECHNIQUES

Dickens uses lots of linguistic techniques in *A Christmas Carol*. You need to analyse techniques in your exam answer to get good marks for AO2.

 It's not enough to just spot techniques. You also need to explain what effect these techniques have on the reader.

Foreshadowing

Foreshadowing is when a writer hints at something that will happen later in the book.

"the houses opposite were mere phantoms"

Comment: Dickens uses this metaphor (see **page 12**) to describe how ghostly the houses look in the fog. However, describing the houses as *"phantoms"* foreshadows the arrival of the ghosts, and creates an eerie and unsettling atmosphere.

Dramatic irony

Dramatic irony describes when the reader knows something that the characters do not.

Comment: In Stave Four, Scrooge overhears a group of businessmen discussing someone who has died. The reader suspects that they are talking about Scrooge, however Scrooge doesn't realise they are talking about him. This creates suspense for the reader as they wonder when Scrooge will realise that he is the dead man.

Symbolism

Symbolism is when an author uses a symbol to represent an idea. Dickens uses warmth to symbolise goodwill and cold to symbolise heartlessness.

Comment: In Stave One, Scrooge has a *"low fire"*, highlighting his miserly nature, whereas Fred is described as being *"a glow"*, which implies he has a warm personality.

Allegory

Allegory is when a text, or an element of a text, has a hidden, bigger meaning.

"This boy is Ignorance. This girl is Want."

Comment: Ignorance and Want aren't just two poor children, they represent the wider problem of poverty. See **page 57** for more.

Foil

A **foil** is a character who is the opposite to another character. Writers use foils to reveal information about one character by contrasting their behaviour and emotions with another.

Comment: Fred acts as a foil to Scrooge. Where Fred is kind and joyful, Scrooge is greedy and miserable. Fred's positive characteristics emphasise just how unpleasant Scrooge is.

Exclamations

Exclamations are sentences which end with an exclamation mark (!), and are used to show strong emotion, such as delight, surprise or fear.

"Oh, glorious! Glorious!"

Comment: In Stave Five, when Scrooge returns to his bedroom after a visit from the Ghost of Christmas Yet to Come, Dickens uses exclamations to show Scrooge's delight at being given a chance to redeem himself.

Rhetorical questions

Rhetorical questions are questions that don't require an answer.

"Scrooge knew he was dead? Of course he did. How could it be otherwise?"

Comment: The narrator uses rhetorical questions to involve the reader and encourage them to acknowledge that Marley was dead.

Sensory language

Sensory language relates to the five senses: sight, touch, smell, taste and sound.

"A smell like an eating-house and a pastrycook's next door to each other, with a laundress's next door to that."

Comment: Dickens' description of the Cratchits' Christmas pudding helps the reader to imagine how good it smells, comparing it to the smell from a baker's and fresh laundry (Christmas puddings were traditionally cooked in fabric).

Alliteration

Alliteration is when words which start with the same sound are grouped closely together in a sentence.

"doomed to wander through the world – oh, woe is me! – and witness what it cannot share"

Comment: Marley's ghost repeats the 'w' sound, which mimics the wailing sound of ghosts, and gives an eerie sound to his words.

Onomatopoeia

Onomatopoeia is when words sound like the noise they are describing.

"Clash, clang... ding, dong"

Comment: In Stave Five, Dickens describes the sound of the church bells. The use of onomatopoeia emphasises the loud and joyful sound they make.

Personification

Personification is when something non-human is described as having human characteristics.

The potatoes *"knocked loudly at the sauce-pan lid to be let out and peeled"*

Comment: Personifying the potatoes makes the scene feel lively and suggests that the potatoes are keen to join the festive celebrations.

Similes

Similes describe something 'like' or 'as' something else.

"chestnuts, shaped like the waistcoats of jolly old gentlemen"

Comment: This creates a positive image of big, round chestnuts, suggesting that they are ripe and sizeable.

Metaphors

Metaphors describe something as being something else.

"He iced his office in the dog days"

Comment: Scrooge has such a cold-hearted temperament that even in the height of summer (the dog days) his office is cold and unwelcoming.

Puns

Puns are a type of wordplay where a word with two meanings creates humour.

"more of gravy than of grave"

Comment: Scrooge thinks Marley's ghost is the result of indigestion. Dickens uses a pun on 'gravy' and 'grave' to show that Scrooge doesn't take Marley's visit seriously.

Humour

Dickens includes moments of comedy to entertain the reader. They are often juxtaposed with dark and sinister moments to provide **comic relief** for the reader.

Juxtaposition is when two contrasting things are placed next to each other for deliberate effect.

"I don't know how long I've been among the Spirits. I don't know anything, I'm quite a baby. Never mind. I don't care. I'd rather be a baby."

Comment: This comical image of Scrooge as a baby is juxtaposed with the end of Stave Four where Scrooge is on his knees begging the Ghost of Christmas Yet to Come to save him. The change of tone from serious to humorous provides comic relief for the reader, and sets a joyful tone at the start of Stave Five.

STAVE ONE

Stave One introduces the character of Scrooge, a miserable and greedy man, who is visited by the ghost of his former business partner, Jacob Marley.

Stave One: Marley's Ghost

Comment: *A Christmas Carol* is told by an unnamed narrator. The narrator often includes his own opinion and speaks in a chatty (by Victorian standards) style, which helps create a sense of familiarity with the reader. For more on the narrator, turn to **page 9**.

The reader is told that Scrooge's business partner, Jacob Marley, is dead: *"Marley was as dead as a door-nail"*.

Comment: Starting the story with death introduces a morbid tone, and hints at the eerie events to come. This establishes the novella as a **ghost story** (see **page 2**). Readers also need to know that Marley is dead so that they are shocked when his ghost appears later in the stave.

The narrator explains the relationship between Scrooge and Marley: Scrooge was Marley's *"sole friend, and sole mourner"*. Despite this, Scrooge *"was not so dreadfully cut up"* by Marley's death, and Scrooge, as an *"excellent man of business"*, commemorated Marley's funeral with *"an undoubted bargain"*.

Comment: This suggests that Marley was not a popular man: only Scrooge attended his funeral, and even Scrooge wasn't particularly upset about Marley's death. Even on the day of Marley's funeral, Scrooge was only concerned about business deals. Marley's lonely funeral **foreshadows** what could happen to Scrooge if he doesn't change his ways.

Scrooge is described as a *"wrenching, grasping, scraping, clutching, covetous old sinner!"*.

Comment: Dickens uses a long list of adjectives to emphasise just how greedy and unpleasant Scrooge is. Establishing Scrooge as a wholly unlikeable character makes his redemption by the end of the novella more astonishing. See **pages 47–49** for more on the theme of redemption.

Scrooge is also presented as unpopular: *"Nobody ever stopped him in the street to say, with gladsome look, "My dear Scrooge, how are you?""*. Even though he knows he is disliked, Scrooge doesn't seem to care or want to change. For more on Scrooge, see **pages 31–33**.

Scrooge is presented as an unlikeable character.

The events of the story begin on Christmas Eve, with Scrooge at work in his *"counting-house"* (accounting firm).

Comment: The narrator begins with the phrase *"Once upon a time"*, which is traditionally the opening line of a fairy tale. Fairy tales usually have a message or a moral, and they often contain magic. Starting the events of the story with this phrase hints there will be similarities between the novella and fairy tales.

Scrooge works in a counting-house.

Outside, it is dark and foggy: *"the fog came pouring in at every chink and keyhole... the houses opposite were mere phantoms"*.

Comment: The darkness and foggy weather add to the mysterious atmosphere. The metaphorical reference to *"phantoms"* **foreshadows** the ghosts that will visit Scrooge. Even though it is Christmas Eve, the setting feels sinister, rather than joyful.

Scrooge's clerk (Bob Cratchit) is introduced. He is working by a small fire that *"looked like one coal"* and he is trying to warm himself by a candle.

Comment: At first, Bob is referred to as the *"clerk"*. He isn't given a name, which shows how little Scrooge cares for him, and how the working class are anonymised.

Bob doesn't ask for more coal on his fire because he fears he would be sacked for asking.

Comment: This shows how poorly Scrooge treats Bob, and how employees in the Victorian era were prepared to endure poor conditions to keep their jobs. The way Scrooge behaves towards Bob contrasts with how Fezziwig treats his staff later in the novella (see **page 19**).

Scrooge's nephew, Fred, enters the counting-house. He is *"cheerful"* and wishes his uncle a merry Christmas. Fred is described as being *"ruddy"* (healthy looking) with eyes that *"sparkle"*.

Comment: Fred acts a **foil** to Scrooge: Fred's joyful and lively demeanour contrasts with Scrooge's miserable nature. However, since they are related, this gives the reader hope that Scrooge can become more like Fred. For more information on Fred, turn to **pages 36–37**.

Scrooge tells Fred that Fred has no reason to be merry because he's poor.

Comment: Scrooge believes that wealth is linked to happiness, and that poor people can't possibly be happy. Fred points out that Scrooge is wealthy, so he should be happy, to which Scrooge replies *"Humbug!"*, implying that no amount of money will make Scrooge happy.

Scrooge thinks Christmas is *"a time for paying bills"*, whereas Fred thinks Christmas is a *"kind, forgiving, charitable, pleasant time"* when people *"think of people below them"*.

Comment: Scrooge's catchphrase is *"Bah, humbug!"*. The word 'humbug' meant 'sham or fraud'. Essentially, Scrooge thinks Christmas is a sham because it doesn't make him any richer. However, Fred sees Christmas as an opportunity to be caring and charitable to those who are less fortunate. For more on the theme of Christmas spirit, turn to **pages 52–53**.

Fred invites Scrooge to have Christmas dinner with him the following day.

Comment: Even though Scrooge is terrible company, Fred still invites Scrooge to have Christmas dinner with him. Fred embodies the generosity of Christmas spirit.

Scrooge rudely declines, telling Fred, *"Good afternoon"*.

Comment: Scrooge cannot even bring himself to wish Fred a Merry Christmas. This shows how little regard Scrooge has for Christmas.

Fred leaves *"without an angry word"*.

As Fred exits, two men enter Scrooge's counting-house. They are collecting money for the *"poor and destitute who suffer greatly"* so that they can buy *"meat and drink, and means of warmth"*.

Comment: In Victorian England, there was little government help for those who lived in poverty, and the poorest members of society had to rely on charity to survive. For more on poverty in Victorian England, turn to **page 6**.

The charity collectors ask Scrooge how much he would like to donate, and he refuses, claiming *"I can't afford to make idle people merry"*. Scrooge believes that people who are *"badly off"* can instead go to the *"prisons"* and *"workhouses"*.

Comment: Workhouses were very unpleasant places. One of the charity collectors admits that *"many would rather die"* than go to a workhouse. For more about Victorian workhouses, turn to **page 7**.

Scrooge tells the charity collectors: *"If they would rather die… they had better do it and decrease the surplus population"*.

Comment: This quote highlights how cold and unfeeling Scrooge is. The Ghost of Christmas Present repeats these words back to Scrooge in Stave Three (see **page 23**).

The charity collectors leave after Scrooge tells them: *"It is enough for a man to understand his own business, and not to interfere with other people's"*.

Comment: Scrooge believes that people are poor because they are lazy, and that they don't deserve help. This was a commonly held perception at the time. See **page 8** for more.

Scrooge finishes work, and begrudgingly tells Bob he can have Christmas Day off, but that he should be *"here all the earlier"* the following day.

Comment: This highlights Scrooge's tight-fisted nature. He is reluctant to give Bob even one day off at Christmas.

Scrooge has dinner in a *"melancholy"* tavern, and then returns to his *"gloomy"* and *"dreary"* home.

Comment: Dickens uses adjectives from the semantic field of sadness and despair to create a vivid impression of Scrooge's miserable life.

Marley's face appears in the doorknocker.

As Scrooge stands at his front door, the doorknocker transforms into Marley's face, with *"ghostly spectacles… on its ghostly forehead"*. The face is *"horrible"*, but it suddenly disappears.

Comment: The ghostly doorknocker is the first supernatural event in the novella, and it **foreshadows** the other ghosts. It also helps to create an unsettling atmosphere for the reader.

Scrooge is *"startled"* and checks the other rooms in his house before double-locking the front door.

Comment: Scrooge is clearly unsettled at seeing Marley's face in the doorknocker. His fear reminds the reader that he is human, and contributes to an atmosphere of suspense.

Scrooge hears bells in house begin to ring. Then just as suddenly, they stop.

Scrooge hears clanking chains from the room beneath him, and the cellar door opens. The ghost of Scrooge's ex-business partner, Jacob Marley, emerges. Marley's ghost is wrapped in a chain made of *"cash-boxes, keys, padlocks, ledgers, deeds, and heavy purses wrought in steel"*.

Comment: The chain wrapped around Marley is a **metaphor** for his greed, and how he is punished in the afterlife for his selfishness when he was alive.

Marley's ghost is stuck in **purgatory** (a place after death where a person experiences suffering), carrying the weight of his chain. Marley's ghost claims Scrooge will have an even longer, heavier chain when he dies, unless he changes his ways.

Comment: Marley's ghost warns Scrooge about the consequences of his greed, but he also tells Scrooge that he has a *"chance and a hope of escaping"* his fate. This creates suspense for the reader, as they wonder whether Scrooge will be able to avoid purgatory.

Marley's ghost, wrapped in chains, visits Scrooge.

Marley's ghost tells Scrooge that he will be visited by *"Three spirits"* who will teach Scrooge how to change his ways.

Comment: Scrooge is unwilling to meet with the spirits, telling Marley's ghost, *"I think I'd rather not"*. This shows that, despite the seriousness of Marley's warning, Scrooge is reluctant to change.

Marley's ghost floats out of the window. Scrooge looks out after him and sees the *"air filled with phantoms"*. The ghosts are all wearing chains and *"moaning"* in an *"inexpressibly sorrowful"* way.

Comment: The phrase *"inexpressibly sorrowful"* suggests that the sound is so sad that Dickens cannot describe it. Instead, the reader must use their own imagination to try to infer the noises the ghosts are making.

Scrooge notes that one of the ghosts *"cried piteously"* because he couldn't help a living woman who was sat with a child on a doorstep. *"The misery with them all was, clearly, that they sought to interfere, for good, in human matters, and had lost the power for ever."*

Comment: The ghosts are tortured in the afterlife by being unable to help the living. Dickens warns his readers that people should help each other when they are alive to avoid being punished after death. Victorian readers would have believed in the ideas of heaven, hell and purgatory, so they would have taken Dickens' warning seriously.

STAVE TWO

Scrooge is visited by the Ghost of Christmas Past, who takes Scrooge back in time to witness several previous Christmases.

Stave Two: The First of the Three Spirits

Scrooge wakes up and hears the church bell chime twelve. Scrooge knows that this clock must be wrong because he went to bed after two.

Comment: The unusual passing of time adds to supernatural atmosphere of the novella.

Scrooge lies in bed and listens to the clock chime one. The curtains around his bed are drawn back by a *"strange figure—like a child: yet not so like a child as like an old man"*. The ghost introduces itself as the Ghost of Christmas Past.

Comment: The ghost speaks to Scrooge using imperative verbs such as *"Take heed!"* and *"Rise! And walk with me!"*. This gives the ghost a sense of authority and urgency as it tries to command Scrooge.

Scrooge is visited by the Ghost of Christmas Past.

The spirit takes Scrooge back in time to the place where Scrooge grew up. The ghost shows Scrooge his younger self: a *"solitary child, neglected by his friends"*.

Comment: Describing Scrooge as *"neglected"* and *"forgotten"* creates sympathy for him, and helps the reader to understand how he has become so bitter.

Scrooge *"sobbed"* when he sees his younger self.

Comment: Scrooge's ability to show emotion gives the reader hope that he is beginning to change. For more on the theme of redemption, turn to **pages 47–49**.

The spirit shows Scrooge another Christmas. This time, Scrooge's sister, Fan, visits Scrooge's boarding school to bring him home. She tells him: *"Father is so much kinder than he used to be"*.

Comment: This hints that Scrooge's father was aggressive, and that Scrooge's childhood was unpleasant. This allows the audience to empathise with Scrooge, and helps to explain why he rejects his only family member, Fred, when he is older.

The spirit reminds Scrooge that his sister had *"a large heart"* and that she died, leaving behind her son, Scrooge's nephew, Fred.

Comment: Scrooge is *"uneasy"* when the spirit reminds him of Fred. This suggests that Scrooge feels guilty for the way that he has treated Fred.

The spirit then shows Scrooge another Christmas. This time, Scrooge is a young man, apprenticed at Mr Fezziwig's warehouse. Mr Fezziwig, Scrooge's boss, hosts a Christmas Eve party with plenty of dancing, food and drink. Fezziwig invites family, friends and employees to the party.

Comment: The party is lively and joyful, and Fezziwig is welcoming and inclusive. Dickens wanted his readers to recognise that employers have a responsibility to take care of their staff, and to use their wealth to benefit others.

The narrator describes how a *"light"* appeared to glow from Fezziwig as he dances.

Comment: Dickens uses light and warmth to symbolise goodness. By describing Fezziwig as bathed in light, Dickens is implying that Fezziwig is a good person.

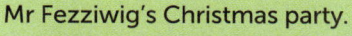

Mr Fezziwig's Christmas party.

The spirit criticises the party: *"A small matter... to make these silly folks so full of gratitude"*. But Scrooge defends Fezziwig: *"The happiness he gives, is quite as great as if it cost a fortune"*.

Comment: The spirit is deliberately critical of Fezziwig so that Scrooge is forced to defend Fezziwig. This encourages Scrooge to admit that happiness is worth more than money.

The spirit urges Scrooge to speak his mind: *"What is the matter?... Something, I think"*. Scrooge replies: *"I should like to be able to say a word or two to my clerk"*.

Comment: This implies that Scrooge is learning from the spirit's visit. Scrooge recognises that he hasn't been a good employer to Bob, and that he wants to make amends.

The ghost tells Scrooge that he doesn't have long: *"My time grows short... Quick!"*

Comment: The ghosts have a limited amount of time with Scrooge. This increases the pace of the story and creates a sense of urgency.

The spirit then shows Scrooge as *"a man in the prime of life"*, but he has begun to look *"greedy"*. He is sitting next to a *"fair young girl"* who has tears in her eyes.

The girl, Belle, tells Scrooge that he has neglected her in favour of a *"golden"* idol (i.e. money) and that he is preoccupied with *"Gain"*. The couple had been engaged when they were *"poor, and content to be so"* but she breaks off the engagement because of Scrooge's obsession with money.

Comment: The spirit shows Scrooge how his greed destroyed his relationship with Belle.

Scrooge is upset by this vision (*"Show me no more!"*) but the spirit forces Scrooge to watch and *"pinioned him in both his arms"*.

Comment: Although the ghost has been quite gentle up until this point, it uses force to make sure that Scrooge learns his lesson. For more on the Ghost of Christmas Past, see **page 41**.

The spirit shows Scrooge what happened to Belle after she broke up with Scrooge. She got married, had a daughter, who herself had several children. Her family is lively, joyful and affectionate. The children are delighted by their father who is *"laden with Christmas toys and presents"*.

Belle's family is lively and joyful.

Comment: The spirit shows Scrooge what his life could have been like if he hadn't prioritised money over love.

Belle's husband was in London and tells Belle that he saw Scrooge *"Quite alone in the world"*.

Comment: Scrooge's isolation contrasts with the lively family. Dickens warns that greed can make people sad and lonely.

Scrooge is upset by what he has seen, telling the ghost: *"Take me back. Haunt me no longer!"*

Comment: Scrooge's reaction suggests he is affected by the vision and is unhappy with the choices that he has made in life. This implies that Scrooge is beginning to change, and he recognises the importance of family and friends.

Scrooge and the ghost wrestle, and Scrooge tries to extinguish the light emitting from the spirit's head, but Scrooge *"could not hide the light"*.

Comment: The light radiating from the ghost symbolises truth. Scrooge's inability to hide the light symbolises how Scrooge cannot hide from his past.

Scrooge returns to his own bedroom, and he falls asleep.

Comment: Scrooge falls asleep easily. This suggests that the ghost's visions haven't affected him enough to keep him awake, and that Scrooge has yet to learn his lesson.

STAVE THREE

Scrooge is visited by the next ghost: the Ghost of Christmas Present.

Stave Three: The Second of the Three Spirits

Scrooge wakes up and sees a *"blaze of ruddy* (red) *light"* in the next room, so he goes to investigate.

Comment: In *A Christmas Carol*, light often symbolises goodwill. The *"ruddy light"* is being produced by the Ghost of Christmas Present, who represents generosity and kindness.

Inside the room, Scrooge sees *"a jolly Giant"* sat next to a *"mighty blaze"* in the fireplace, surrounded by holly, mistletoe and ivy, as well as plates of *"red-hot chestnuts, cherry-cheeked apples, juicy oranges"*. The ghost introduces itself as the Ghost of Christmas Present. It holds a *"glowing torch"* and wears a holly wreath around its head.

Here, the word 'torch' refers to a flaming stick of wood. Torches were used to give light before the invention of electricity. The ghost's torch symbolises how he 'lights the way' for Scrooge.

Comment: The Ghost of Christmas Present is similar in appearance to Jesus. The holly wreath could be a reference to Jesus' crown of thorns. Since most Victorians were religious, likening the ghost to Jesus would have made its message seem more important. See **page 42** for more.

Scrooge tells the ghost: *"if you have aught to teach me, let me profit by it"*.

Comment: Scrooge talks *"submissively"* to the spirit, which suggests he respects the ghost and is prepared to learn from the visit. Scrooge's attitude towards the ghosts is changing.

The spirit takes Scrooge to the poorer part of London where *"the shortest streets were choked up with a dingy mist"*. However, there was *"an air of cheerfulness"*.

Comment: The spirit tries to show Scrooge that even the poorer members of society are cheerful, and that money cannot buy happiness.

The Ghost of Christmas Present shows Scrooge several Christmas celebrations.

Scrooge and the ghost watch people take their food to *"the baker's shop"*.

Some families couldn't afford to cook at home because coal was so expensive. Instead, they took their food to a bakery to be cooked.

The ghost *"sprinkled incense"* on people's dinners using its torch.

Comment: The ghost uses its torch to bless people, food and homes. The blessings spread goodwill and Christmas cheer.

The ghost blesses poor people most often because they need *"it the most"*.

Comment: The ghost challenges the idea that the poor only have themselves to blame. The ghost believes that the poorest members of society deserve help.

Scrooge asks the spirit why he deprives them *"of their means of dining every seventh day"*.

Comment: Dickens was critical of **Sabbatarianism** (observing Sunday as a holy day). Businesses, such as bakeries, were closed on Sundays, which meant the poor couldn't have their food heated. A law was passed in 1836 which also prohibited recreation on Sundays. Dickens felt that this was unfair as it prevented working-class people from being able to enjoy themselves on their day off.

The ghost tells Scrooge: *"There are some upon this earth of yours... who lay claim to know us, and do their deeds of passion, pride, ill-will, hatred, envy bigotry and selfishness in our name... charge their doings on themselves, not us."*

Comment: This is another example of the Ghost of Christmas Present being linked to Jesus. The ghost tells Scrooge that religion should not be blamed for those people who behave in an unchristian way. Dickens uses the ghost to criticise those people who claim to be Christians, but do not treat others with kindness and compassion.

Scrooge and the ghost visit Bob Cratchit's house. They see Bob's wife dressed *"poorly in a twice-turned gown, but brave in ribbons"*.

Comment: Bob's wife's dress is described as *"twice turned"*. This means the dress has been thoroughly worn, then unstitched and sewn back together in-side out to make it look new again. She then decorated it with *"ribbons"* to try to make it look pretty. This signifies how the Cratchit family are poor, but they try to make the best of their situation.

The ghost and Scrooge visit the Cratchits' house.

The Cratchit family work together to prepare Christmas dinner. The scene is lively and joyful and the *"young Cratchits danced about the table"*.

Comment: Dickens presents the Cratchits positively, showing their loving, happy and hardworking nature. Dickens wanted to challenge the idea that the working class were lazy and unpleasant. For more on the Cratchit family, turn to **page 40**.

Bob and his son, Tiny Tim, enter. Tiny Tim has *"a little crutch... his limbs supported by an iron frame"*.

Although Tiny Tim is unwell, he doesn't complain. This highlights the resilience of the poor, and evokes sympathy from the reader. For more on Tiny Tim, see **page 40**.

The family eat Christmas dinner which is *"Eked out by apple-sauce and mashed potatoes"*.

Comment: The Cratchits bulk out their Christmas dinner with cheap ingredients, like apples and potatoes, because they cannot afford a larger, more expensive goose.

Scrooge asks the ghost, *"tell me if Tiny Tim will live"*. The ghost replies: *"If these shadows remain unaltered by the Future, the child will die"*. Scrooge is saddened by the ghost's response. The ghost repeats Scrooge's words from Stave One: *"If he be like to die, he had better do it, and decrease the surplus population"*.

Comment: Scrooge's interest in Tiny Tim shows that he is beginning to develop compassion towards others. Scrooge is ashamed to hear the ghost repeat his own words back at him, which suggests that Scrooge's attitude towards the poor is changing.

Bob Cratchit makes a toast to Scrooge as the *"Founder of the Feast"*.

Comment: Bob calls Scrooge the *"Founder of the Feast"* because Scrooge has paid for Christmas dinner via the wages he pays Bob. This shows Bob's kind nature. Even though Scrooge treats him badly, Bob recognises that his employer helps him to support his family. For more on the character of Bob, turn to **page 39**.

Mrs Cratchit is dismayed by Bob's toast. She calls Scrooge *"an odious, stingy, hard, unfeeling man"*, and *"the mention of his name cast a dark shadow on the party"*.

Comment: Even though the family rely on Bob's job at Scrooge's counting-house, they recognise that Scrooge is not a fair employer and that he treats Bob badly.

Scrooge and the ghost leave the Cratchits' house and walk through the streets seeing *"every house expecting company, and piling its fires half-chimney high"*. The ghost then takes Scrooge to a *"cheerful"* family of miners, then to see two lighthouse keepers who wish each other *"Merry Christmas"* and finally to a ship where *"every man on board... remembered those he cared for at a distance"*.

Comment: Dickens shows the reader different groups of people celebrating Christmas to emphasise that family and kindness are the most important elements of Christmas. For more on the theme of Christmas spirit, turn to **pages 52−53**.

The ghost takes Scrooge to Fred's house. Fred and his wife are laughing at Scrooge calling Christmas *"a humbug"*. Fred admits that Scrooge is *"not so pleasant as he might be. However ... I have nothing to say against him."*

Comment: This highlights Fred's kind nature. Even though Scrooge has treated him poorly, Fred refuses to say a bad word against him. For more on the character of Fred, turn to **pages 36−37**.

Scrooge and the ghost watch Fred and his family listen to music, play games, and raise a toast to Scrooge. Upon watching the toast, Scrooge became *"light of heart"*.

Comment: Watching Fred's Christmas celebrations causes Scrooge to realise the joy of Christmas and the benefit of spending time with his family.

The spirit takes Scrooge to *"sick beds"*, an *"almshouse"* (charitable housing) and a *"jail"* to bless people celebrating Christmas.

Comment: Dickens doesn't describe these visits in detail. This increases the pace of the story as it creates the impression that time is speeding up, and Scrooge is hurtling towards his fate.

Scrooge notices that the ghost is growing *"clearly older"*, and the spirit confirms that its life will end that evening at midnight.

Comment: Unlike the other two ghosts, the Ghost of Christmas Present grows old and dies. This suggests that the present is fleeting, and that people should make the most of life while they can.

Scrooge notices a *"claw"* beneath the spirit's robes, and the ghost unveils two *"frightful, hideous and miserable"* children. The spirit tells Scrooge they are mankind's children: Ignorance and Want.

Ignorance and Want are an example of **allegory**. See page 10 for more.

Comment: Ignorance and Want are represented as malnourished and poverty-stricken children. Dickens deliberately juxtaposes their description with the merry Christmas scenes beforehand to remind the audience that poverty is a serious societal problem that exists all year round.

The spirit warns Scrooge about Ignorance and Want, but says, *"beware most of all"* Ignorance.

Comment: Dickens warns his readers that keeping the poor 'ignorant' (i.e. uneducated) would lead to the *"Doom"* of mankind. He believed that giving the poor an education was the key to breaking the cycle of poverty.

Comment: The ghost's language changes when he warns Scrooge. The ghost's speech becomes more urgent, using imperative verbs *"Beware"*, *"Deny"*, *"Slander"* and *"Admit"*, as well as using exclamations to show his strength of feeling.

Scrooge asks: *"Have they no refuge or resource?"*. Again, the ghost uses Scrooge's own words against him, replying: *"Are there no prisons? ... Are there no workhouses?"*

Comment: Dickens uses the ghost to voice his own criticisms against wealthy Victorians who were unwilling to help those less fortunate.

As the church bell strikes midnight, the Ghost of Christmas Present disappears and the next ghost arrives: *"a solemn Phantom, draped and hooded"*.

Comment: This time, Scrooge doesn't go back to his house to await the final ghost, instead it appears just as the Ghost of Christmas Present fades away. This increases the pace of the story, and suggests that time is running out for Scrooge to learn his lesson.

STAVE FOUR

The final ghost visits Scrooge: The Ghost of Christmas Yet to Come. The spirit shows what the future has in store for Scrooge and the Cratchit family.

Stave Four: The Last of the Spirits

The final ghost approaches, and *"Scrooge bent down upon his knee"*.

Comment: The act of bending down on your knee is a sign of submission. This shows how Scrooge's reaction to the ghosts have changed. He respects the final ghost, and is willing to listen and learn.

The ghost's appearance is mysterious. It is *"shrouded in a deep black garment, which concealed its head, its face, its form"* and its presence fills Scrooge with *"solemn dread"*.

Comment: This description may remind readers of the Grim Reaper (death). This sinister ghost contrasts with the Ghost of Christmas Present who was happy and full of life, and creates a sombre and fearful atmosphere. For more, see **page 43**.

The ghost does not speak, but Scrooge knows that it is the Ghost of Christmas Yet to Come, who will show Scrooge *"shadows of the things that have not happened but will happen in the time before us"*.

Scrooge acknowledges: *"I hope to live to be another man from what I was"*.

Comment: Even before the ghost has shown Scrooge the future, he is prepared to change.

The spirit takes Scrooge into London, where he listens to a group of businessmen talking. They talk uncaringly about someone's death (*"I thought he'd never die"*) and his funeral (*"I'll go if lunch is provided"*). Scrooge doesn't realise the businessmen are talking about his future self.

Comment: This creates **dramatic irony** for the reader, and makes them wonder when Scrooge will realise that he is the dead man. The uncaring way the businessmen talk about Scrooge also serves as a warning to the audience: if you live a life of selfishness, people will not respect your memory when you die.

The spirit takes Scrooge to a different part of London full of *"crime, ... filth and misery"* and shows him a pawn shop where *"old rags, bottles, bones and greasy offal, were bought"*.

Comment: Dickens' wealthier readers might not have been familiar with the realities of London's slums. The description of the neighbourhood is shocking, and highlights the awful conditions that some people lived in.

Three people enter the pawn shop, each with a *"heavy bundle"*. They have stolen items from Scrooge's house, including his bed curtains, and are trying to sell them to the pawn broker, Old Joe.

Comment: The three thieves have jobs: a *"charwoman"* (cleaner), *"laundress"* and an *"undertaker's man"*. This implies that even though these people are employed, they still need to turn to crime to make ends meet.

One of the women says: Scrooge died: *"gasping out his last there, alone by himself"*.

Comment: The image of Scrooge *"gasping"* on his deathbed alone and unloved is unpleasant, and warns the reader of the consequences of selfish behaviour.

The three thieves do not feel remorse for stealing Scrooge's possessions.

Comment: This vision suggests that Scrooge's wealth and possessions will fall into the wrong hands after his death, rather than benefitting honest people, like the Cratchits or Fred.

Scrooge still doesn't realise that he is the dead man, but he recognises that *"the case of this unhappy man might be my own"*. He is affected by the vision, *"shuddering from head to foot"*.

The spirit takes Scrooge to the man's deathbed, where a corpse is lying, *"unwatched, unwept, uncared for"*. A sheet covers its face, which hides its identity.

Comment: Even at this point, Scrooge still doesn't realise that he is the dead man. This builds tension, as the reader wants to know how Scrooge will react when he discovers the truth.

Scrooge asks the spirit to show him someone who felt emotion at the man's death, and the spirit shows him a family who owed Scrooge money, and were relieved to hear he was dead so that they had more time to pay off their debts. The family comment they will *"sleep to-night with light hearts"*.

Dickens had first-hand experience of the consequences of unpaid debts. His father was imprisoned for not keeping up with loan repayments.

Scrooge asks the spirit to show him *"some tenderness connected with a death"*. The spirit takes him to the Cratchits' house, where the family are mourning the loss of Tiny Tim. Bob Cratchit has just returned from visiting Tiny Tim's gravesite, and he *"broke down all at once"*.

Comment: Tiny Tim, unlike Scrooge, is mourned and loved when he dies, despite being poor and living a much shorter life. Dickens suggests that being a good person is more important than being wealthy.

Bob tells his family that he bumped into Fred who asked about Tiny Tim's passing. Fred offered to help Bob and his family. Mrs Cratchit calls Fred a *"good soul"*.

Comment: Mrs Cratchit's opinion of Fred contrasts with her opinion of Scrooge in Stave Three.

Scrooge still doesn't realise he is the dead man, and asks the spirit: *"Let me behold what I shall be, in days to come."* The spirit takes him to a churchyard which is *"overrun by grass and weeds"*.

Comment: The place where Scrooge is buried is neglected and uncared for, emphasising how he has been forgotten.

Scrooge asks the ghost: *"Are these the shadows of the things that Will be, or are they shadows of things that May be, only"*.

Comment: Scrooge wants to know if it's too late to change the course of his fate. He recognises that he needs to change, but wants assurance that it's not too late.

The ghost points to a grave where Scrooge's name is written. Scrooge finally realises that he was the dead man in the bed, and he is distraught. He clutches the ghost's robe and tells him: *"I am not the man I was. I will not be the man I must have been"*.

Comment: Dickens reinforces Scrooge's fear and distress as he pleads with the Ghost of Christmas Yet to Come. This show of emotion would have been quite shocking to Victorian readers, as society expected people to behave in a reserved and polite manner.

The ghost *"shrunk, collapsed and dwindled down into a bedpost"*.

STAVE FIVE

Scrooge wakes in his bedroom on Christmas morning and is a changed man.

Stave Five: The End of It

Comment: The tone of Stave Five is joyful and optimistic. This sharply contrasts with the end of Stave Four which saw Scrooge on his knees pleading with the Ghost of Christmas Yet to Come. The **juxtaposition** of different tones creates variety and interest for the reader.

Scrooge wakes up in his bed, and is delighted that the *"Time before him was his own, to make amends in!"*

Comment: Scrooge immediately wants to make changes in his life, suggesting that he has learnt from the ghosts' visits.

Scrooge comments that he is *"as happy as an angel, I am as merry as a schoolboy. I am as giddy as a drunken man"*.

Comment: The way Scrooge talks and behaves in Stave Five is dramatically different to how he is presented in Stave One. The repetition in *"I am as happy as an angel, I am as merry as a schoolboy. I am as giddy as a drunken man"* highlights Scrooge's excitement and delight.

Scrooge hears the bells ringing: *"Clash, clang, hammer; ding, dong, bell"*.

Comment: The use of **onomatopoeia** reinforces the joyful, lively atmosphere.

Scrooge puts his head out of the window and there is *"No fog, no mist; clear, bright, jovial"*.

Comment: Just like Scrooge, the weather has changed. The fog from Stave One has been replaced by a clear, bright day. The weather mirrors Scrooge's new-found optimism.

Scrooge calls to a boy on the street and asks what day it is. The boy replies *"Why, Christmas Day."*

Comment: Only a few hours have passed since Scrooge was visited by Marley's ghost. This adds to the supernatural nature of the story, as it feels as though much more time has passed.

Scrooge tells the boy to buy the *"prize Turkey"* that was hanging in the butcher's window, and he arranges for it to be sent it to Bob Cratchit's house anonymously. Scrooge chuckles as he pays for the turkey and its delivery.

Comment: Dickens repeats the word *"chuckle"* to emphasise Scrooge's joyful mood.

Scrooge leaves his house and greets everyone with a *"delighted smile"*. He meets the charity collectors, and donates a large sum of money: *"a great many back-payments are included in it"*.

Comment: Scrooge tries to rectify a lifetime of greed.

Scrooge then goes to visit Fred: *"He passed the door a dozen times, before he had the courage to go up and knock"*.

Comment: Scrooge is hesitant because he is embarrassed by the way he has treated Fred in the past.

When he enters Fred's house, Fred is delighted to see his uncle: *"It is a mercy he didn't shake his arm off"*. The narrator describes the Christmas celebrations as: *"Wonderful Party, wonderful games, wonderful unanimity, won-der-ful happiness"*.

Comment: Dickens repeats the word *"wonderful"* to emphasise Scrooge's positive transformation.

Scrooge spends Christmas Day with Fred and his wife.

The next day, Scrooge goes to his office early. Bob is eighteen minutes late for work. At first, Scrooge pretends to be angry, but then he gives Bob a pay rise. Bob is so shocked, he contemplates going to *"the court for help and a strait-waistcoat"* (straitjacket, a jacket used to restrain someone).

Comment: Bob thinks that Scrooge has gone mad and that he needs restraining with a straitjacket. This reminds the reader of the transformation that Scrooge has undergone.

Scrooge tells Bob that not only will he raise his salary, but he will also *"endeavour to assist your struggling family"*.

Comment: Scrooge asks Bob to *"Make up the fires"*. In *A Christmas Carol*, fires, light and warmth symbolise goodwill, so Scrooge's request contrasts with the meagre fires in the office in Stave One and emphasises his new, generous personality.

The narrator finally summarises that thanks to Scrooge's help, Tiny Tim did not die, and Scrooge *"became as good a friend, as good a master, and as good a man, as the good old city knew"*.

Comment: Dickens wanted his wealthy readers to experience the same transformation as Scrooge, and to become more charitable to those less fortunate. Dickens explains how Scrooge's generosity saves Tiny Tim's life, suggesting that generosity and compassion could make the difference between life and death to those struggling with poverty.

The final line of the novella is *"God bless Us, Every One!"*.

Comment: This line reinforces the importance of Christian values to Victorian readers, and also reminds audiences that everyone, no matter whether rich or poor, deserves kindness.

CHARACTERS: EBENEZER SCROOGE

Scrooge's character completely changes over the course of the novella. He starts out as a cruel miser, and transforms into a loving and generous man.

Stave One

Comment: Dickens spends most of Stave One establishing Scrooge as an unlikeable character with no redeeming features. This creates suspense for the audience as it seems unlikely that he will be able to change, and makes his eventual transformation much more satisfying.

Greedy: Scrooge only cares about work and making money. He's described as *"a tight-fisted hand at the grindstone"*.

Comment: The image of Scrooge being *"tight-fisted"* emphasises how he holds on to money and refuses to let go. The phrase *"hand at the grindstone"* suggests that Scrooge is preoccupied with work.

In Stave One, Scrooge is an unlikeable character.

Isolated: Scrooge doesn't have any friends, and he rejects his only family member, Fred. The narrator describes Scrooge as: *"secret, and self-contained, and solitary as an oyster"*.

Comment: The **alliteration** of the 's' sound in this quote creates a hissing sound, reinforcing Scrooge's unpleasant nature. However, oysters sometimes contain pearls. This hints that there could be goodness hidden within Scrooge too.

Cold-hearted: He doesn't care about anyone else, and his uncaring nature shows on his face: *"The cold within him froze his old features"*.

Comment: Dickens uses cold and heat symbolically throughout the novella. Dickens uses language from the semantic field of cold to represent Scrooge's miserly attitude, whereas he uses heat and fire to represent generosity, such as the Ghost of Christmas Present's torch.

Unsympathetic: Scrooge has little sympathy for the poor. He tells the charity collectors that the workhouses and prisons *"cost enough; and those who are badly off must go there"*.

Comment: Scrooge believes that enough is already being done to help the poorest members of society through taxes which pay for the workhouses and prisons. He begrudges paying taxes, and he doesn't believe that the poor deserve charity. For more on attitudes towards the poor, turn to **page 8**.

··· Ebenezer Scrooge, Stave One continued

Doubtful: When Marley's ghost appears, Scrooge doesn't believe what he sees. He thinks Marley might be *"an undigested bit of beef"*.

Some people believed that eating a large meal late at night could cause bad dreams. Scrooge thinks the ghost could just be a nightmare caused by a late dinner.

Comment: Scrooge is cynical towards Marley's ghost. This contrasts with the respect he shows the other ghosts later in the novella, which highlights how much Scrooge has changed.

Fearful: When Scrooge doesn't take him seriously, Marley's ghost lets out a *"frightful cry"* and removes the bandage around his head, which causes his jaw to fall down. Scrooge *"fell upon his knees, and clasped his hands before his face"*.

Comment: Scrooge's fear reminds the reader of his human side. This gives the reader hope that Scrooge has the ability to change.

Scrooge is initially doubtful when Marley's ghost appears.

Stave Two

Emotional: When the Ghost of Christmas Past takes Scrooge to his childhood town, Scrooge is emotional: his *"lip is trembling"*, his *"cold eye"* glistens and he is *"filled with gladness"*.

Comment: This *"gladness"* is caused by Scrooge listening to people wishing each other 'Merry Christmas'. This **foreshadows** Scrooge's happiness on Christmas Day in Stave Five.

Lonely: The Ghost of Christmas Past shows Scrooge as a *"solitary child, neglected by his friends"*.

Comment: This suggests that Scrooge had an unhappy childhood, and his loneliness helps to explain how he became so cold-hearted. The visions from Scrooge's childhood show how he wasn't always unpleasant, implying that he has the capacity to be a good person again.

Greedy: The spirit shows how Belle broke off her engagement to Scrooge because he was too focused on making money. This vision is painful for Scrooge to watch, and he calls it *"torture"*.

Comment: Scrooge tells Belle there is nothing *"so hard as poverty"*. This suggests that Scrooge fears being poor. This could explain his greed: he hoards money to protect himself from ever suffering from poverty.

Stave Three

Respectful: When the Ghost of Christmas Present visits Scrooge, Scrooge behaves *"submissively"*, and says *"if you have aught to teach me, let me profit by it"*.

Comment: Scrooge's reaction contrasts with his reluctance to meet the ghosts in Stave One, when he asks Marley's ghost: *"Couldn't I take 'em all at once, and have it over, Jacob?"*. This suggests that he is beginning to recognise the importance of the ghosts' visits.

Caring: Scrooge becomes attached to Tiny Tim *"with an interest he had never felt before"*.

Comment: Tiny Tim evokes Scrooge's compassion, and makes him realise that many people suffer through no fault of their own.

Shocked: When Scrooge sees Ignorance and Want, he is *"appalled"* by their appearance. He asks, *"Have they no refuge or resource?"*, showing that he wants them to be looked after.

Comment: The ghost replies using Scrooge's own words against him: *"Are there no prisons?"*. The ghost implies that it is selfish people like Scrooge who are stopping the poor from getting the help that they need.

Stave Four

Frightened: Scrooge is afraid of the Ghost of Christmas Yet to Come: *"I fear you more than any spectre I have seen"*.

Comment: Scrooge is most frightened of this ghost because it will show him his future. Scrooge recognises that his future will be unpleasant if he doesn't change his ways.

Ignorant: For most of this stave, Scrooge doesn't realise that the man who has died is his future self.

Comment: This is an example of **dramatic irony**. Scrooge's ignorance increases the suspense as the reader wonders when he will realise, and what his reaction will be.

Scrooge becomes *"a second father"* to Tiny Tim.

Stave Five

Changed: Scrooge is *"glowing with good intentions"*.

Comment: The word *"glowing"* has connotations of warmth, which contrasts with the descriptions of him as *"cold"* in Stave One. This shows the inward change that has occurred.

Generous: He sends an enormous turkey to the Cratchits' house, makes a large donation to charity, and gives Bob a pay rise.

Comment: Scrooge's transformation is complete. He's no longer the miserable, greedy man from the start of the novella.

In this extract from the beginning of Stave Five, Scrooge has just woken up in his bedroom following a visit from the Ghost of Christmas Yet to Come.

YES! and the bedpost was his own. The bed was his own, the room was his own. Best and happiest of all, the Time before him was his own, to make amends in!

"I will live in the Past, the Present, and the Future!" Scrooge repeated, as he scrambled out of bed. "The Spirits of all Three shall strive within me. Oh Jacob Marley! Heaven, and the Christmas Time be praised for this! I say it on my knees, old Jacob; on my knees!"

He was so fluttered and so glowing with his good intentions, that his broken voice would scarcely answer to his call. He had been sobbing violently in his conflict with the Spirit, and his face was wet with tears.

"They are not torn down," cried Scrooge, folding one of his bed-curtains in his arms, "they are not torn down, rings and all. They are here—I am here—the shadows of the things that would have been, may be dispelled. They will be. I know they will!"

His hands were busy with his garments all this time; turning them inside out, putting them on upside down, tearing them, mislaying them, making them parties to every kind of extravagance.

"I don't know what to do!" cried Scrooge, laughing and crying in the same breath; and making a perfect Laocoön* of himself with his stockings. "I am as light as a feather, I am as happy as an angel, I am as merry as a schoolboy. I am as giddy as a drunken man. A merry Christmas to everybody! A happy New Year to all the world. Hallo here! Whoop! Hallo!"

He had frisked into the sitting-room, and was now standing there: perfectly winded.

"There's the saucepan that the gruel was in!" cried Scrooge, starting off again, and going round the fireplace. "There's the door, by which the Ghost of Jacob Marley entered! There's the corner where the Ghost of Christmas Present, sat! There's the window where I saw the wandering Spirits! It's all right, it's all true, it all happened. Ha ha ha!"

Really, for a man who had been out of practice for so many years, it was a splendid laugh, a most illustrious laugh. The father of a long, long line of brilliant laughs!

"I don't know what day of the month it is!" said Scrooge. "I don't know how long I've been among the Spirits. I don't know anything. I'm quite a baby. Never mind. I don't care. I'd rather be a baby. Hallo! Whoop! Hallo here!"

He was checked in his transports by the churches ringing out the lustiest peals he had ever heard. Clash, clang, hammer; ding, dong, bell. Bell, dong, ding; hammer, clang, clash! Oh, glorious, glorious!

Running to the window, he opened it, and put out his head. No fog, no mist; clear, bright, jovial, stirring, cold; cold, piping for the blood to dance to; Golden sunlight; Heavenly sky; sweet fresh air; merry bells. Oh, glorious! Glorious!

* Laocoön — a figure from Greek and Roman mythology who was entangled by giant snakes. Scrooge is comparing himself and his stockings to the snakes that wrapped themselves around Laocoön.

Starting with this extract, explore how Dickens presents ideas about joy and happiness.

Write about:
- how Dickens presents joy and happiness in this extract
- how Dickens presents ideas about joy and happiness in the novel as a whole. [30]

Your answer may include:

AO1 — show understanding of the text
- *Scrooge is joyful because the visions shown by the Ghost of Christmas Yet to Come have not come true, and he has been given the opportunity to "make amends" and redeem his past behaviour of greed and selfishness.*
- *This extract juxtaposes with the previous stave where Scrooge was pleading with the Ghost of Christmas Yet to Come. This joyful opening to Stave Five contrasts with the ominous and desperate tone of Stave Four, emphasising Scrooge's joy and relief.*
- *Scrooge is so excited and joyful he struggles to dress himself, putting his clothes on "upside down". This comical image is the exact opposite of Scrooge's character from Stave One, where he is sombre and miserable, which emphasises the extent of Scrooge's transformation. This gives the reader hope that Scrooge has changed for good.*
- *Elsewhere in the novella, joy and happiness are associated with family and companionship. For example, Dickens shows the joy of the Cratchit family as they gather for Christmas, and the joyful atmosphere at Fezziwig's Christmas party.*

AO2 — show understanding of the writer's language choices
- *Energetic verbs such as "scrambled" and "frisked" show Scrooge's eagerness and happiness.*
- *Exclamations show Scrooge's delight, suggesting that he is shouting and cannot contain his excitement: "Hallo here! Whoop! Hallo!"*
- *Onomatopoeia in the sounds of the bells ringing: "Clash, clang, hammer, ding, dong". This sensory imagery creates the impression of a joyful, lively morning.*
- *Fragmented sentences show how Scrooge's thoughts are racing due to his excitement: "clear, bright, jovial. Stirring cold".*

AO3 — relate the novella to the context
- *Dickens wanted to make Scrooge's redemption clear to the reader. Scrooge's change of character provides a satisfying ending, and suggests that even the most selfish person is capable of change.*
- *Dickens wanted his readers to appreciate that compassion for others can bring happiness. He believed that kindness and generosity could create a fairer, happier society.*
- *Prior to Scrooge's redemption, Dickens shows how poorer characters, such as the Cratchits, are happier than Scrooge, even though they struggle to make ends meet. This suggests that family brings more happiness than wealth and material possessions.*

This answer should be marked in accordance with the levels-based mark scheme on page 61.

Make sure your answer to this question is in paragraphs and full sentences.
Bullet points have been used in this example answer to suggest some information you could include.

CHARACTERS: FRED

Fred is Scrooge's nephew. Even though Scrooge is unpleasant to Fred, Fred never stops treating his uncle with kindness.

Stave One

Comment: Fred acts as a **foil** to Scrooge. Fred's kind and cheerful nature emphasises Scrooge's miserly and unpleasant ways.

Joyful: Fred greets Scrooge with a "cheerful voice".

Comment: Fred is described as having *"a glow"* and his eyes *"sparkle"*. This emphasises Fred's warm and lively personality, and contrasts with the cold atmosphere in Scrooge's office.

Scrooges tries to push Fred away in Stave One.

Poor: Scrooge tells Fred, *"What reason have you to be merry? You're poor enough"*.

Comment: Even though Fred isn't wealthy, he's happier than Scrooge. Fred admits: *"There are many things from which I might have derived good, by which I have not profited"*. Dickens uses the character of Fred to show that wealth doesn't bring happiness. This also reinforces Scrooge's greed: Scrooge knows his nephew is poor, but doesn't offer to help him.

Compassionate: Fred recognises that Christmas is: *"a kind, forgiving, charitable, pleasant time"*.

Comment: Fred shows compassion, and he embodies Christmas spirit. For more on the theme of Christmas spirit, turn to **pages 52–53**.

Determined: Even though Scrooge is openly dismissive and hostile towards him, Fred keeps trying to reach out to his uncle: *"I ask nothing of you; why cannot we be friends?"*.

Comment: Fred's relentless optimism is admirable. Just like Marley and the ghosts, he doesn't want to give up on Scrooge.

Stave Three

Fred's home is described as *"bright"* and *"gleaming"*.
It is warm and welcoming, just like Fred.

Good-humoured: Fred is *"blest"* (blessed) with a hearty laugh, and is amused by Scrooge calling Christmas *"a humbug"*.

Comment: The narrator comments that he is *"unlikely"* to find someone *"blest"* with a better laugh than Fred. The narrator includes his own opinion to highlight Fred's good nature.

Forgiving: Fred says of Scrooge: *"I couldn't be angry with him if I tried"*, and *"I mean to give him the same chance every year"*.

Comment: Even the Ghost of Christmas Present, who spreads Christmas joy with a torch, looks at Fred with *"approving affability"*: the ghost admires Fred's goodwill.

Stave Four

Generous: When he learns of Tiny Tim's death, Fred offers to help the Cratchit family.

Comment: Even though Fred isn't wealthy and doesn't know the Cratchits well, he still wants to help them. The Cratchits are very grateful for Fred's offer, showing how the smallest acts of kindness can make an impression.

Stave Five

Welcoming: When Scrooge visits Fred on Christmas Day, Scrooge felt right *"at home in five minutes"*.

Comment: Fred's Christmas is described as *"Wonderful party, wonderful games, wonderful unanimity, won-der-ful happiness!"*. The repetition of *"wonderful"* emphasises Fred's generous hospitality.

CHARACTERS: JACOB MARLEY

Jacob Marley was Scrooge's business partner, but he died seven years previously. Marley's ghost suffers in the afterlife because of his greed, and he warns Scrooge he must change his ways, or he will suffer a similar fate.

Stave One

Dead: The narrator makes it very clear from the outset that *"Marley was dead"*.

> **Comment:** Dickens repeatedly mentions Marley's death to make Marley's ghostly reappearance more shocking. The reference to death also creates an unsettling atmosphere at the start of the novella.

Marley appears before Scrooge, wrapped in a chain.

Isolated: Scrooge was Marley's *"sole friend, and sole mourner"*. Just like Scrooge, Marley didn't have any close relationships with friends or family and distanced himself from others.

> **Comment:** Dickens highlights the similarities between Scrooge and Marley to suggest that Scrooge will suffer the same fate as Marley unless he learns compassion.

Greedy: Marley wears a *"long"* chain made of *"cash-boxes, keys, padlocks, ledgers, deeds and heavy purses wrought in steel"*.

> **Comment:** The chain that Marley wears was *"forged in life"*. This means it is a punishment for his greed when he was alive. Marley's ghost warns that Scrooge's chain is even longer: *"It was full as heavy and as long as this, seven Christmas Eves ago"*. This suggests that Scrooge has been even greedier than Marley, so Scrooge's fate will be even worse.

Regretful: Marley's ghost is tortured in the afterlife because of his greed. He *"cannot rest"* and is tormented by the lack of compassion he showed in life.

> **Comment:** Scrooge sees a group of phantoms outside who try to *"interfere, for good, in human matters, and had lost the power for ever"*. The ghosts' punishment for their greed is being unable to help those who are suffering.

Selfless: Marley visits Scrooge to warn him about the consequences of greed. It's implied that Marley has arranged for the three ghosts to visit Scrooge to try to help him *"shun the path I tread"*.

> **Comment:** Even though Marley has nothing to gain by Scrooge's redemption, Marley's ghost wants Scrooge to change before it's too late.

CHARACTERS: BOB CRATCHIT

Bob Cratchit is Scrooge's clerk, and head of the Cratchit family. He has a wife and several children, including his son, Tiny Tim.

Stave One

Tolerant: Bob works in poor conditions in Scrooge's counting-house. His workspace is *"dismal"* and he's so cold in the office he tries to *"warm himself at the candle"*.

> **Comment:** As poor as the conditions are, Bob doesn't complain because he doesn't want to lose his job. It's implied his family wouldn't be able to survive without his salary.

Poor: Scrooge pays Bob *"fifteen shillings a week"* which is barely enough to provide for his family. He wears a *"comforter"* (scarf) to keep himself warm because he can't afford a coat.

> **Comment:** Scrooge is very rich, whereas Bob barely makes ends meet. Scrooge exploits Bob for his own gain. Dickens highlights the division between rich and poor. For more on the class system, see **pages 4–5**.

Friendly: He speaks *"cordially"* to Fred, and on his way home from the office he *"went down a slide"* (sliding on the ice) twenty times with some local children.

> **Comment:** Unlike Scrooge, who miserably eats a *"melancholy dinner"* after work, Bob is fun-loving and playful. Dickens shows that even though Bob is poor, he still finds joy in life.

Bob carries Tiny Tim home from church.

Stave Three

Loving: Bob is an affectionate father. He *"hugged his daughter until his heart's content"*.

> **Comment:** Bob values his family. Family was very important to Victorians, so this makes his character more sympathetic and likeable to readers.

Stave Four

Grieving: In the vision shown to Scrooge by the Ghost of Christmas Yet to Come, Tiny Tim dies, and Bob *"walked a little slower than he used"*.

> **Comment:** Even though Bob no longer carries Tiny Tim on his shoulders, he walks slower than before. This shows how the grief at losing his son has affected him. Despite his sorrow, Bob tries to stay positive in front of the rest of his family.

CHARACTERS: THE CRATCHIT FAMILY

Dickens uses the Cratchit family to show his readers that people who live in poverty aren't nameless: they are real families who experience real hardships.

The Cratchit family

Comment: The Cratchits are hard-working and treat each other with kindness, which encourages the reader to empathise with them. Dickens wanted his readers to recognise that poverty affects families, like the Cratchits, through no fault of their own.

The Cratchits are presented as a loving family.

Hard-working: The family work hard to make Christmas dinner. Mrs Cratchit makes the gravy, Peter mashes the potatoes, Belinda sweetens the apple sauce and Martha dusts the hot plates: the family help each other and work together.

Comment: The description of the meal preparation also creates a sense of bustle and energy, giving the Cratchit household a lively and festive atmosphere.

Content: Even though the Christmas dinner is bulked up with *"apple sauce and mashed potatoes"* and the Christmas pudding is very small for such a large family, the Cratchits express their *"universal admiration"* for the meal.

Comment: Rather than wishing they had more, the family are grateful and appreciate what they have. This contrasts with Scrooge's greed.

Tiny Tim

Well-behaved: Bob describes Tiny Tim as *"good as gold"*.

Comment: Although this idiom means Tiny Tim was *'well behaved'*, Dickens' choice of language suggests that, to Bob, family is just as important as gold.

Religious: Tiny Tim believes that Jesus *"made lame beggars walk, and blind men see"*.

Comment: Christianity was important to the Victorians, so Tiny Tim's faith would have been admirable to 19th-century readers.

Uncomplaining: Even though he is unwell, Tiny Tim doesn't complain about his illness.

Comment: Tiny Tim's positivity contrasts with Scrooge's miserable demeanour.

CHARACTERS: THE GHOST OF CHRISTMAS PAST

The Ghost of Christmas Past takes Scrooge back in time and shows him as a boy and a young man.

Comment: The ghosts are very different, both in terms of how they look and how they act. This creates interest for the reader, and also allows Dickens to incorporate different elements of symbolism into their appearances and personalities.

Stave Two

Contradictory: The ghost is described as *"like a child: yet not so like a child as like an old man"*.

> **Comment:** The childlike nature of the ghost could symbolise innocence, whereas the elderly nature could symbolism wisdom.

Illuminated: There is a *"bright clear jet of light"* shining from the ghost's head.

> **Comment:** This light could symbolise truth. Scrooge begs the ghost to cover his head, which implies that Scrooge isn't initially prepared to see the truth.

The Ghost of Christmas Past visits Scrooge first.

Helpful: Scrooge wonders why the spirit has visited him, and the spirit says, *"Your welfare"* and *"Your reclamation"*.

> **Comment:** The ghost's purpose is to help Scrooge become a better man.

Enquiring: The ghost questions Scrooge: *"what is that upon your cheek?"*, *"You recollect the way?"*, *"What is the matter?"*.

> **Comment:** The ghost uses questions to encourage Scrooge to engage with the visions and talk about his emotions. The ghost wants Scrooge to learn from his visit.

Forceful: When Scrooge is reluctant to see the vision of Belle's family, the ghost *"pinioned"* (restrained) Scrooge and forces him to watch.

> **Comment:** The ghost makes sure that Scrooge watches and learns from the visions. It's committed to Scrooge's redemption.

CHARACTERS: THE GHOST OF CHRISTMAS PRESENT

The Ghost of Christmas Present shows Scrooge different Christmas celebrations. The ghost carries a torch, which it uses to bless people.

Stave Two

Comment: The ghost wears a scabbard (a sheath for a sword) but there is no blade in it, and the scabbard is *"eaten up with rust"*. This implies that the ghost is associated with peace.

Cheerful: The ghost is described as *"jolly"*, with a *"cheery voice"* and it welcomes Scrooge, saying: *"Come in, and know me better"*.

Comment: The Ghost of Christmas Present is friendly and welcoming. It contrasts with the mysterious, sinister Ghost of Christmas Yet to Come, who appears afterwards.

Christ-like: The description of the ghost reminds the reader of Jesus. It is barefoot, wears a wreath of holly (similar to Jesus' crown of thorns) and it has *"dark brown curls"* that are *"long and free"*.

Comment: Most Victorian readers would have been religious, so likening the ghost to Christ would have made the message of goodwill and compassion seem more meaningful.

The Ghost of Christmas Present shows Scrooge the meaning of goodwill.

Compassionate: The ghost *"sprinkled incense"* on passers-by. The incense acts as a blessing, and spreads goodwill and cheer.

Comment: The ghost sympathises with the poor. It challenges the idea that poor people do not deserve help and kindness.

Flippant: The ghost uses Scrooge's words against him. When the ghost reveals Ignorance and Want, and Scrooge asks, *"Have they no refuge or resource?"* the ghost retorts *"Are there no prisons?... Are there no workhouses?"*, words which Scrooge spoke to the charity collectors in Stave One.

Comment: Hearing his own words used against him makes Scrooge realise how callous he was.

CHARACTERS: THE GHOST OF CHRISTMAS YET TO COME

The Ghost of Christmas Yet to Come is silent and terrifying.

Stave Three

Unlike the other two ghosts, the Ghost of Christmas Yet to Come doesn't fetch Scrooge from his house. Instead, the spirit arrives just as the Ghost of Christmas Present disappears. This increases the pace of the story, highlighting the urgency of the ghost's visit, and the inevitability of the future.

Stave Four

Mysterious: The ghost moves *"slowly, gravely"* and Scrooge never sees its face because it is *"shrouded in a deep black garment, which concealed its head, its face, its form"*.

Comment: The ghost's mysterious appearance symbolises how the future is also unknown.

The Ghost of Christmas Yet to Come resembles the Grim Reaper, a skeleton shrouded in a black, hooded robe. The Grim Reaper is the personification of death.

Silent: The ghost does not speak, instead it *"inclined its head"* or points.

Comment: The ghost's silence adds to its mysterious and ominous nature. It also means that Scrooge cannot rely on the spirit to tell him the importance of what has been shown. Scrooge must understand the meaning of the visions himself.

The Ghost of Christmas Yet to Come shows Scrooge his grave.

Frightening: Scrooge is so frightened of the ghost he *"can hardly stand"*.

Comment: The Ghost of Christmas Yet to Come shows Scrooge visions of a frightening future. The ghost uses fear to try to encourage Scrooge to change his ways.

In this extract from Stave Two, the Ghost of Christmas Past shows Scrooge a Christmas party held by his old employer, Mr Fezziwig.

A positive light appeared to issue from Fezziwig's calves. They shone in every part of the dance like moons. You couldn't have predicted, at any given time, what would have become of them next. And when old Fezziwig and Mrs. Fezziwig had gone all through the dance; advance and retire, both hands to your partner, bow and curtsey, corkscrew, thread-the-needle, and back again to your place; Fezziwig "cut"—cut so deftly, that he appeared to wink with his legs, and came upon his feet again without a stagger.

When the clock struck eleven, this domestic ball broke up. Mr. and Mrs. Fezziwig took their stations, one on either side of the door, and shaking hands with every person individually as he or she went out, wished him or her a Merry Christmas. When everybody had retired but the two 'prentices, they did the same to them; and thus the cheerful voices died away, and the lads were left to their beds; which were under a counter in the back-shop.

During the whole of this time, Scrooge had acted like a man out of his wits. His heart and soul were in the scene, and with his former self. He corroborated everything, remembered everything, enjoyed everything, and underwent the strangest agitation. It was not until now, when the bright faces of his former self and Dick were turned from them, that he remembered the Ghost, and became conscious that it was looking full upon him, while the light upon its head burnt very clear.

"A small matter," said the Ghost, "to make these silly folks so full of gratitude."

"Small!" echoed Scrooge.

The Spirit signed to him to listen to the two apprentices, who were pouring out their hearts in praise of Fezziwig: and when he had done so, said,

"Why! Is it not? He has spent but a few pounds of your mortal money: three or four perhaps. Is that so much that he deserves this praise?"

"It isn't that," said Scrooge, heated by the remark, and speaking unconsciously like his former, not his latter, self. "It isn't that, Spirit. He has the power to render us happy or unhappy; to make our service light or burdensome; a pleasure or a toil. Say that his power lies in words and looks; in things so slight and insignificant that it is impossible to add and count 'em up: what then? The happiness he gives, is quite as great as if it cost a fortune."

He felt the Spirit's glance, and stopped.

"What is the matter?" asked the Ghost.

"Nothing particular," said Scrooge.

"Something, I think?" the Ghost insisted.

"No," said Scrooge, "No. I should like to be able to say a word or two to my clerk just now. That's all."

Starting with this extract, explore how Dickens uses the ghosts to help Scrooge change his attitudes and behaviours.

Write about:
- how Dickens uses the Ghost of Christmas Past in this extract
- how Dickens uses the ghosts to help Scrooge change his attitudes and behaviours in the novel as a whole.
[30]

Your answer may include:

AO1 — show understanding of the text

- *The Ghost of Christmas Past shows Scrooge how Fezziwig treats everyone with kindness. Fezziwig shakes "hands with everybody individually", including Scrooge's past self. Scrooge recognises the positive impact that Fezziwig's generosity has on those around him.*

- *This vision helps Scrooge to acknowledge that he should treat Bob Cratchit with more kindness. Scrooge comments: "I should like to be able to say a word or two to my clerk".*

- *The other ghosts show Scrooge visions to try to change his attitudes and behaviours. The Ghost of Christmas Yet to Come presents Scrooge with the consequences of a life of greed, whereas the Ghost of Christmas Present shows Scrooge the Cratchits' Christmas to highlight the importance of family and the idea that wealth does not bring happiness.*

AO2 — show understanding of the writer's language choices

- *Dickens uses light to describe Fezziwig: a "positive light appeared to issue from Fezziwig's calves". This symbolises Fezziwig's goodness and generosity.*

- *Dickens uses the phrase "pouring out their hearts in praise". The heart has connotations of love, so this emphasises the strength of love that younger Scrooge felt towards Fezziwig.*

- *The ghost questions Scrooge to elicit a response from him: "What's the matter?" and "Something I think?", encouraging Scrooge to reflect on his past behaviour.*

AO3 — relate the novella to the context

- *Dickens uses this extract to highlight that employers have the power to make their employees happy. Dickens believed that better pay and working conditions could help to alleviate some societal problems, such as poverty.*

- *Dickens uses the other ghosts to highlight other societal issues. For example, the Ghost of Christmas Present shows Ignorance and Want to highlight how a lack of education can trap people in a cycle of poverty. Dickens wanted his readers to recognise that reform was needed to bring about societal change.*

- *The ghost story genre allows Dickens to use supernatural elements to convey his messages. For example, he uses the phantoms in Stave One to suggest that the punishment for greed was torment in the afterlife.*

This answer should be marked in accordance with the levels-based mark scheme on page 61.

 Make sure your answer to this question is in paragraphs and full sentences.
Bullet points have been used in this example answer to suggest some information you could include.

CHARACTERS: IGNORANCE AND WANT

Ignorance and Want are two impoverished children that are revealed from the Ghost of Christmas Present's robes. They are allegorical, and represent how society has created poverty.

Comment: Ignorance and Want only appear briefly in Stave Four, but they are an important symbol of social injustice in the Victorian era. Dickens wanted his readers to reflect on what could be done to tackle poverty.

Stave Four

Comment: Presenting Ignorance and Want as children makes their characterisation more shocking, and generates more sympathy from the audience.

Silent: Ignorance and Want do not speak.

Comment: This symbolises how the poor are often voiceless, and must rely on others in society to help them.

Scrooge meets Ignorance and Want.

Hidden: The children are concealed inside the Ghost of Christmas Present's robe.

Comment: This symbolises how societal problems, such as poverty, are hidden away or ignored by the public.

Neglected: They are described as *"Yellow, meagre, ragged"*.

Comment: Describing their skin tone as *"Yellow"* suggests that they are ill. The word *"meagre"* implies they are weak and malnourished, and *"ragged"* suggests they are wearing rags, that are insufficient to keep them warm in winter. Their appearance would have reminded readers of poverty-stricken children.

Unpleasant: They are *"scowling, wolfish"*.

Comment: The word *"scowling"* suggests that they are angry at how they have been treated, and *"wolfish"* implies an animal aggression, suggesting that they could be dangerous. This description implies that they have been dehumanised by poverty.

Dangerous: The Ghost of Christmas Present warns Scrooge, *"Beware them both... but most of all beware this boy, for on his brow I see that written which is Doom"*.

Comment: Dickens warns the reader that a lack of education amongst the poor (i.e. ignorance) is a danger to society. Dickens believed that education could help poor people break free from poverty by allowing them to access better-paid employment.

THEMES: REDEMPTION

Over the course of the novella, Scrooge sees the damage caused by his cold-hearted and selfish attitude. He learns from the ghosts' messages, and is given a second chance to turn his life around.

Scrooge

The novella revolves around Scrooge's redemption. Scrooge is initially presented as greedy and unpleasant. The ghosts show Scrooge how his greed hurts those around him, such as Bob and Belle. By the end of the novella, Scrooge pledges to make amends for his past, and to change for the better.

Comment: Although Scrooge has led a life of selfishness, Dickens suggests that it is never too late for someone to change. Dickens wanted his readers to realise that they also had the opportunity for redemption, irrespective of their past behaviour.

Marley's ghost

Marley's ghost visits Scrooge and warns that he will be punished in the afterlife if he doesn't change. This creates dramatic tension for the reader, as they wonder if Scrooge will change or if he will suffer in purgatory like Marley.

Comment: Victorian society was very religious and believed in the concepts of heaven and hell. Suggesting that those people who behave uncharitably in life would be punished in the afterlife would have encouraged readers to reflect on their own compassion towards the poor.

Marley's warning isn't enough to convince Scrooge to change, and he is initially reluctant to meet with the ghosts.

Comment: Scrooge's initial scepticism is in-keeping with his character. It also creates suspense for the reader as it's unclear whether Scrooge will learn his lesson.

Scrooge seems reluctant to change following his visit from Marley's ghost.

The Ghosts

Over the course of the novella, the ghosts try to teach Scrooge lessons about the importance of family and generosity. These lessons help Scrooge redeem himself.

Comment: Scrooge's redemption is gradual. He is initially wary of the Ghost of Christmas Present and tries to extinguish the spirit's light when he becomes upset. However, he slowly realises that he must learn from the spirits if he wants to change.

The Ghost of Christmas Past shows Scrooge the importance of family.

Importance of family

Each of the ghosts show Scrooge visions of family: both his own family, and other people's. The ghosts try to impress upon Scrooge the value of family, and the happiness that family brings.

The Ghost of Christmas Past shows Scrooge his sister, Fan, and reminds him of her loving nature and *"large heart"*. The ghost also reminds Scrooge that Fred is Scrooge's sole living relative. The ghost shows Scrooge that Belle found happiness by becoming a wife and raising a family.

The Ghost of Christmas Present shows the Cratchits celebrating Christmas. They are *"happy, grateful, pleased with one another"*, demonstrating to Scrooge that happiness comes from spending time as a family, rather than wealth and possessions.

The Ghost of Christmas Present shows Scrooge that if he doesn't change, he will die alone and *"unwatched, unwept, uncared for"*.

Comment: Although the ghosts show Scrooge visions which encourage him to change, Scrooge recognises that the change needs to come from within.

Importance of generosity

The ghosts show Scrooge the effects of generosity and greed.

The Ghost of Christmas Past shows Scrooge Fezziwig's party. Scrooge realises that Fezziwig only spent a few pounds on the party, but that the *"happiness he gives, is quite as great as if it costs a fortune"*. This helps Scrooge to realise that small acts of kindness can have a big impact on others.

The Ghost of Christmas Present shows Scrooge Ignorance and Want. They highlight the consequences of living selfishly, and not having compassion for those who are less fortunate.

The Ghost of Christmas Yet to Come shows Scrooge that without his intervention, Tiny Tim dies. This demonstrates how generosity can make the difference between life and death.

Comment: In Stave One, Scrooge is isolated and miserable. By Stave Five, Scrooge reaches out to those around him, and this compassion brings him joy. Dickens suggests that being kind and generous leads to happiness.

Dickens uses a symmetrical structure to encourage the reader to compare Scrooge's behaviour in the first and final staves. He does this by repeating Scrooge's interactions with Bob, Fred and the charity collectors to show how much Scrooge has changed. This is a satisfying resolution to the novella, as it shows the reader how Scrooge has made amends and reassures the reader that Scrooge's transformation is permanent.

Comment: When Scrooge changes his behaviour and becomes selfless and generous, his demeanour also changes, and he becomes happier and more light-hearted. For example, *"he chuckled until he cried"* and walking through the streets brings him *"so much happiness"*. Dickens is keen to highlight to the reader that acting selflessly brings a person happiness.

Scrooge learns the importance of compassion.

Stave One

Bob Cratchit

Bob is treated poorly, and paid very little. Bob is afraid that Scrooge will fire him if he steps out of line.

Fred

Scrooge treats Fred rudely, and rejects his nephew's offer of friendship. He dismisses Christmas as *"humbug"*.

Charity collectors

Scrooge refuses to donate to charity, because he thinks his taxes already do enough to help the poor.

Stave Five

Bob Cratchit

Scrooge raises Bob's salary, and offers to help Bob's family. He becomes a *"second father"* to Bob's son, Tiny Tim. Scrooge has learnt the importance of being a generous employer.

Fred

Scrooge visits Fred on Christmas Day and has a *"Wonderful party"*. Scrooge has learnt the value of family and appreciates the spirit of Christmas.

Charity collectors

Scrooge donates a large sum to charity including a *"great many back-payments"*, suggesting that Scrooge wants to make amends for his past behaviour, and now recognises his duty to help those who are less fortunate.

In this extract from Stave One, Scrooge is visited by Marley's ghost, who tells Scrooge that he will be visited by three spirits.

"You will be haunted," resumed the Ghost, "by Three Spirits."

Scrooge's countenance fell almost as low as the Ghost's had done.

"Is that the chance and hope you mentioned, Jacob?" he demanded, in a faltering voice.

"It is."

"I—I think I'd rather not," said Scrooge.

"Without their visits," said the Ghost, "you cannot hope to shun the path I tread. Expect the first to-morrow, when the bell tolls One."

"Couldn't I take 'em all at once, and have it over, Jacob?" hinted Scrooge.

"Expect the second on the next night at the same hour. The third upon the next night when the last stroke of Twelve has ceased to vibrate. Look to see me no more; and look that, for your own sake, you remember what has passed between us!"

When it had said these words, the spectre took its wrapper from the table, and bound it round its head, as before. Scrooge knew this, by the smart sound its teeth made, when the jaws were brought together by the bandage. He ventured to raise his eyes again, and found his supernatural visitor confronting him in an erect attitude, with its chain wound over and about its arm.

The apparition walked backward from him; and at every step it took, the window raised itself a little, so that when the spectre reached it, it was wide open.

It beckoned Scrooge to approach, which he did. When they were within two paces of each other, Marley's Ghost held up its hand, warning him to come no nearer. Scrooge stopped.

Not so much in obedience, as in surprise and fear: for on the raising of the hand, he became sensible of confused noises in the air; incoherent sounds of lamentation and regret; wailings inexpressibly sorrowful and self-accusatory. The spectre, after listening for a moment, joined in the mournful dirge; and floated out upon the bleak, dark night.

Scrooge followed to the window: desperate in his curiosity. He looked out.

The air was filled with phantoms, wandering hither and thither in restless haste, and moaning as they went. Every one of them wore chains like Marley's Ghost; some few (they might be guilty governments) were linked together; none were free. Many had been personally known to Scrooge in their lives. He had been quite familiar with one old ghost, in a white waistcoat, with a monstrous iron safe attached to its ankle, who cried piteously at being unable to assist a wretched woman with an infant, whom it saw below, upon a door-step. The misery with them all was, clearly, that they sought to interfere, for good, in human matters, and had lost the power for ever.

Whether these creatures faded into mist, or mist enshrouded them, he could not tell. But they and their spirit voices faded together; and the night became as it had been when he walked home.

Scrooge closed the window, and examined the door by which the Ghost had entered. It was double-locked, as he had locked it with his own hands, and the bolts were undisturbed. He tried to say "Humbug!" but stopped at the first syllable. And being, from the emotion he had undergone, or the fatigues of the day, or his glimpse of the Invisible World, or the dull conversation of the Ghost, or the lateness of the hour, much in need of repose; went straight to bed, without undressing, and fell asleep upon the instant.

Starting with this extract, explore how Dickens presents ideas about redemption in *A Christmas Carol*.

Write about:
- how Dickens presents redemption in this extract
- how Dickens presents ideas about redemption in the novel as a whole. [30]

Your answer may include:

AO1 — show understanding of the text
- *Marley's ghost warns Scrooge about the consequences of greed, and encourages him to change his ways so that he can redeem himself and avoid punishment in the afterlife.*
- *The phantoms are "unable to assist a wretched woman", suggesting that the punishment for greed and selfishness is being unable to help people who suffer.*
- *Initially, Scrooge is reluctant to change and doesn't recognise the seriousness of Marley's warning. When Marley tells Scrooge he will be visited by the spirits who will teach Scrooge how to redeem himself, Scrooge replies: "I think I'd rather not".*
- *Elsewhere in Stave One, Scrooge is presented as wholly unlikeable and unpleasant. This creates suspense for the reader as Scrooge seems beyond redemption.*
- *By the end of the novella, Scrooge has been redeemed into a charitable and kind-hearted person who shows compassion. Dickens wanted to show how even the most selfish people are capable of redemption.*

AO2 — show understanding of the writer's language choices
- *Marley's ghost uses imperatives to express the seriousness of his message to Scrooge. For example. He says, "Expect" and "Look" and uses exclamations to try to command Scrooge.*
- *Scrooge tries to say the word "Humbug" but he stops himself. This suggests that Scrooge is already starting to change as he decides against criticising what he has just witnessed.*
- *Dickens uses language from the semantic field of sadness to describe the phantoms. They make "incoherent sounds of lamentation and regret" and "cried piteously". This highlights how the ghosts suffer and are punished in the afterlife. The word "incoherent" suggests that the sounds are indescribably awful. This suggests that Scrooge will suffer a terrible fate unless he redeems himself.*

AO3 — relate the novella to the context
- *Victorian readers would have been Christians and familiar with the idea of heaven and hell. Readers would have been frightened by the idea that greed is punished in the afterlife.*
- *Dickens wanted to encourage readers to act with compassion. He uses Scrooge to show that even the most selfish people are capable of redemption.*
- *Using the ghost story genre allows Dickens to show an alternative future where Scrooge does not redeem himself, and dies "unwatched, unwept, uncared for". This demonstrates the consequences of greed and the importance of change and redemption.*

This answer should be marked in accordance with the levels-based mark scheme on page 61.

Make sure your answer to this question is in paragraphs and full sentences.
Bullet points have been used in this example answer to suggest some information you could include.

THEMES: CHRISTMAS SPIRIT

If someone has 'Christmas spirit' it means they act with kindness, generosity and happiness. Dickens thought people should show Christmas spirit all year round.

Christmas and Christianity

Although Christmas is a Christian celebration, Dickens focuses on the secular (non-religious) aspects of the holiday, for example, Christmas dinner, time with family and party games.

Dickens acknowledges that not everyone who claims to be a Christian acts with compassion. Instead, Dickens believes that happiness, kindness and generosity should be part of a person's human nature, rather than being associated with someone's religious beliefs.

Comment: Setting the story over the Christmas period allows Dickens to contrast Scrooge's unpleasant, miserly character with the goodwill of others, making his character seem even more unsympathetic.

The majority of Dickens' Victorian readers would have been very familiar with Christmas, so setting the novel at this time of year allows readers to reflect on their own behaviour during the festive period, and consider how they could embody the Christmas spirit all year round.

The charity collectors

The charity collectors show Christmas spirit by raising money to help those who cannot afford to celebrate Christmas. The charity collectors see Christmas as a time when *"Want is keenly felt and Abundance rejoices"*. They recognise that Christmas highlights the division between the rich and the poor, and they want to help those who are struggling.

Fred

Fred embodies Christmas spirit: he is welcoming, charitable and cheerful. Fred describes Christmas as a time when men and women should *"open their shut-up hearts freely, and think of people below them"*. Even though Scrooge initially pushes Fred away, Fred doesn't hold a grudge against him, and welcomes Scrooge into his house on Christmas Day.

Fezziwig

Fezziwig shows Christmas spirit when he throws his party. He provides food, drink and music for the guests, highlighting his generosity. He shakes hands with each guest, reinforcing his warm and welcoming nature.

Scrooge acknowledges that although Fezziwig only spent a *"few pounds"* on the party, the happiness he spread was *"as if it cost a fortune"*. Scrooge recognises that making people happy is more valuable than money.

The Ghost of Christmas Present

The Ghost of Christmas Present represents Christmas spirit. The ghost is *"jolly"* and *"glorious to see"*.

> **Comment:** The Ghost of Christmas Present is associated with fire and warmth. The ghost sits next to a *"mighty blaze"* and holds a *"glowing torch"* which *"shed its light on Scrooge"*. Throughout the novel, Dickens uses fire and heat to symbolise goodwill and kindness.

The Ghost of Christmas Present embodies Christmas spirit

The Ghost of Christmas Present shows Scrooge lots of different Christmases, but focuses on Christmas celebrations of the working class. The ghost takes Scrooge to a poor part of London, where the people are *"jovial"* and *"full of glee"*. The ghost wants to show Scrooge the poor can enjoy Christmas despite their poverty.

The ghost carries a torch which is used to bless homes and spread goodwill. The spirit sprinkles water on people and their food, especially the poor, because they need *"it most"*.

> **Comment:** The spirit shows compassion to the poor, encouraging readers to do the same.

The Cratchits

The Cratchits also show Christmas spirit. They treat each other with affection (Bob hugs Martha *"to his heart's content"*) and kindness (the dinner is complimented with *"universal admiration"*). For the Cratchits, Christmas is a chance to spend time together as family.

Scrooge

By the end of the novella, Scrooge is full of Christmas spirit. He makes several generous gestures: he buys a turkey for the Cratchits and donates a large sum of money to the charity collectors. The narrator confirms that Scrooge continued to act with Christmas spirit every year after: *"it was always said of him, that he knew how to keep Christmas well"*.

"My dear sir," said Scrooge, quickening his pace, and taking the old gentleman by both his hands. "How do you do? I hope you succeeded yesterday. It was very kind of you. A merry Christmas to you, sir!"

"Mr. Scrooge?"

"Yes," said Scrooge. "That is my name, and I fear it may not be pleasant to you. Allow me to ask your pardon. And will you have the goodness"—here Scrooge whispered in his ear.

"Lord bless me!" cried the gentleman, as if his breath were taken away. "My dear Mr. Scrooge, are you serious?"

"If you please," said Scrooge. "Not a farthing less. A great many back-payments are included in it, I assure you. Will you do me that favour?"

"My dear sir," said the other, shaking hands with him. "I don't know what to say to such munifi—"

"Don't say anything, please," retorted Scrooge. "Come and see me. Will you come and see me?"

"I will!" cried the old gentleman. And it was clear he meant to do it.

"Thank'ee," said Scrooge. "I am much obliged to you. I thank you fifty times. Bless you!"

He went to church, and walked about the streets, and watched the people hurrying to and fro, and patted children on the head, and questioned beggars, and looked down into the kitchens of houses, and up to the windows, and found that everything could yield him pleasure. He had never dreamed that any walk—that anything—could give him so much happiness. In the afternoon he turned his steps towards his nephew's house.

He passed the door a dozen times, before he had the courage to go up and knock. But he made a dash, and did it:

"Is your master at home, my dear?" said Scrooge to the girl. Nice girl! Very.

"Yes, sir."

"Where is he, my love?" said Scrooge.

"He's in the dining-room, sir, along with mistress. I'll show you up-stairs, if you please."

"Thank'ee. He knows me," said Scrooge, with his hand already on the dining-room lock. "I'll go in here, my dear."

He turned it gently, and sidled his face in, round the door. They were looking at the table (which was spread out in great array); for these young housekeepers are always nervous on such points, and like to see that everything is right.

"Fred!" said Scrooge.

Dear heart alive, how his niece by marriage started! Scrooge had forgotten, for the moment, about her sitting in the corner with the footstool, or he wouldn't have done it, on any account.

"Why bless my soul!" cried Fred, "who's that?"

"It's I. Your uncle Scrooge. I have come to dinner. Will you let me in, Fred?"

Let him in! It is a mercy he didn't shake his arm off. He was at home in five minutes. Nothing could be heartier. His niece looked just the same. So did Topper when he came. So did the plump sister when she came. So did every one when they came. Wonderful party, wonderful games, wonderful unanimity, won-der-ful happiness!

Starting with this extract, explore how Dickens presents ideas about joy and happiness in *A Christmas Carol*.

Write about:

- how Dickens presents joy and happiness in this extract
- how Dickens presents ideas about joy and happiness in the novel as a whole. [30]

Your answer may include:

AO1 — show understanding of the text

- *This extract from Stave Five follows Scrooge's redemption. He is joyful because he has been given a second chance to make amends and redeem his greedy and selfish past.*
- *Scrooge finds happiness from donating money to charity, spending time with Fred, as well as simply walking around the streets of London. Dickens suggests that happiness comes from generosity and family, as well as simply enjoying life, rather than from money or possessions.*
- *This is echoed elsewhere in the novel. For example, Dickens also shows joy and happiness from the generosity of Fezziwig's Christmas party as well the joy of the Cratchit's Christmas celebrations as they spend time as a family.*

AO2 — show understanding of the writer's language choices

- *In the lines "He went to church, and walked about the streets, and watched the people hurrying to and fro, and patted children on the head..." Dickens repeats the conjunction "and" in the long list of actions to express Scrooge's bustling activity and his new-found enthusiasm for the simple things in life, that bring him "so much happiness".*
- *The exaggeration of "It is a mercy he didn't shake his arm off" expresses just how delighted Fred is to see Scrooge, and how spending time with family brings Fred joy.*
- *The repetition of "wonderful" in the phrase "Wonderful party, wonderful games, wonderful unanimity, won-der-ful happiness" emphasises how happy Scrooge is.*
- *Dickens' use of exclamation marks throughout the extract ("Bless you!") to show the characters' positivity and enthusiasm in their dialogue. This gives the extract an excited and buoyant tone.*

AO3 — relate the novella to the context

- *Dickens shows how acting with Christmas spirit helps to spread joy and happiness. Dickens wanted readers to embody Christmas spirit all year round.*
- *Dickens wants his readers to recognise that generosity can lead to happiness, for both the giver and the receiver. When Scrooge was greedy and miserly he was miserable and unhappy, but when he acts with kindness and generosity, Scrooge not only makes himself happy, but also the charity collector and Fred.*
- *Dickens believed that compassion and generosity could help to alleviate societal problems, such as poverty. Dickens uses the novella to encourage readers to behave in a selfless way.*

This answer should be marked in accordance with the levels-based mark scheme on page 61.

Make sure your answer to this question is in paragraphs and full sentences.
Bullet points have been used in this example answer to suggest some information you could include.

THEMES: POVERTY

Dickens wanted his readers to acknowledge the social injustice in Britain at the time, and for people to show more compassion to the less fortunate.

Poverty was a particularly serious issue in Victorian Britain. Turn to **page 6** for more.

The charity collectors

The theme of poverty is introduced in Stave One when the charity collectors visit Scrooge to ask for a donation. The charity collectors imply that the poor cannot afford necessities, such as *"meat and drink, and means of warmth"*. This suggests that the government are not doing enough to help those in poverty who *"suffer greatly"*.

Scrooge thinks that he already does enough to help the poor by paying taxes which fund prisons, workhouses and the treadmill (see **page 7**). Scrooge believes that the poor deserve harsh treatment and punishment because they are *"idle"*. He also comments that they are the *"surplus population"*, implying that impoverished people are unworthy of life.

Comment: This opinion was shared by some Victorians who resented paying taxes which helped the poor. Dickens presents Scrooge's opinions as selfish and cold-hearted to show his disapproval of those who do not behave charitably.

The Cratchit family

The Cratchit family represent the poor working class. Dickens presents them positively; they are loving, hardworking and grateful for what they have.

Comment: Dickens presents them in this way to generate sympathy from the audience, and to challenge the stereotype that the poor were lazy and amoral.

Bob works for Scrooge, but he is treated poorly. Bob is paid very little and expected to work in cold, *"dismal"* conditions.

The family live in a four-roomed house, whereas Scrooge lives in a large apartment all to himself. Dickens wanted to highlight how even the most hard-working people can struggle to make ends meet if they are not paid fairly.

The novella implies that Tiny Tim's ill-health can be resolved with financial help: when Scrooge becomes a *"second father"* to Tiny Tim, he doesn't die. Dickens suggests that if society is willing to help the poor, it can make the difference between life and death.

Without help from Scrooge, Tiny Tim dies in the future.

Ignorance and Want

Ignorance and Want personify mankind's selfishness and uncaring attitude towards the poor. Want represents those living in poverty, and Ignorance represents how a lack of education traps the poor in a cycle of poverty. The Ghost of Christmas Present warns that Ignorance will lead to *"Doom"*: the spirit implies that society could crumble if the cycle of poverty is not broken.

Comment: Dickens presents Ignorance and Want as children to provoke a response from his readers. Children are often synonymous with innocence, suggesting that Ignorance and Want have been abandoned and left to suffer through no fault of their own. It also implies that they are too young to help themselves.

Old Joe and the Thieves

In Stave Four, the Ghost of Christmas Yet to Come shows Scrooge three thieves who have stolen the dead man's possessions and are trying to sell them to a pawn broker, Old Joe. The pawn broker's shop is in a part of London where the streets are *"foul and narrow"* and reek of *"filth"* and *"misery"*. Dickens doesn't shy away from describing the terrible conditions that some people lived in, or the reality that some people had to turn to crime to make ends meet.

Comment: Dickens recognises that poverty is connected to other societal problems such as unsanitary conditions and crime.

The thieves have stolen items that aren't worth much, including *"a brooch of no great value"* and *"a pair of sleeve buttons"*. This shows how desperate the thieves are for money.

The thieves do not feel guilty for robbing the dead man, claiming they have a *"right to take care of themselves"*.

Comment: Some readers may have been shocked by the thieves' lack of respect towards the dead man. However, the thieves show a similar attitude to Scrooge in Stave One when Scrooge says: *"It's enough for a man to understand his own business, and not to interfere with other people's"*. Dickens implies that the thieves' lack of compassion isn't that different from the wealthy's lack of compassion towards the poor.

In this extract from Stave Four, Scrooge and the Ghost of Christmas Yet to Come visit a pawn shop.

They left the busy scene, and went into an obscure part of the town, where Scrooge had never penetrated before, although he recognised its situation, and its bad repute. The ways were foul and narrow; the shops and houses wretched; the people half-naked, drunken, slipshod, ugly. Alleys and archways, like so many cesspools, disgorged their offences of smell, and dirt, and life, upon the straggling streets; and the whole quarter reeked with crime, with filth, and misery.

Far in this den of infamous resort, there was a low-browed, beetling shop, below a pent-house roof, where iron, old rags, bottles, bones, and greasy offal, were bought. Upon the floor within, were piled up heaps of rusty keys, nails, chains, hinges, files, scales, weights, and refuse iron of all kinds. Secrets that few would like to scrutinise were bred and hidden in mountains of unseemly rags, masses of corrupted fat, and sepulchres* of bones. Sitting in among the wares he dealt in, by a charcoal stove, made of old bricks, was a grey-haired rascal, nearly seventy years of age; who had screened himself from the cold air without, by a frousy curtaining of miscellaneous tatters, hung upon a line; and smoked his pipe in all the luxury of calm retirement.

Scrooge and the Phantom came into the presence of this man, just as a woman with a heavy bundle slunk into the shop. But she had scarcely entered, when another woman, similarly laden, came in too; and she was closely followed by a man in faded black, who was no less startled by the sight of them, than they had been upon the recognition of each other. After a short period of blank astonishment, in which the old man with the pipe had joined them, they all three burst into a laugh.

"Let the charwoman alone to be the first!" cried she who had entered first. "Let the laundress alone to be the second; and let the undertaker's man alone to be the third. Look here, old Joe, here's a chance! If we haven't all three met here without meaning it!"

"You couldn't have met in a better place," said old Joe, removing his pipe from his mouth. "Come into the parlour. You were made free of it long ago, you know; and the other two an't strangers. Stop till I shut the door of the shop. Ah! How it skreeks! There an't such a rusty bit of metal in the place as its own hinges, I believe; and I'm sure there's no such old bones here, as mine. Ha, ha! We're all suitable to our calling, we're well matched. Come into the parlour. Come into the parlour."

The parlour was the space behind the screen of rags. The old man raked the fire together with an old stair-rod, and having trimmed his smoky lamp (for it was night), with the stem of his pipe, put it in his mouth again.

While he did this, the woman who had already spoken threw her bundle on the floor, and sat down in a flaunting manner on a stool; crossing her elbows on her knees, and looking with a bold defiance at the other two.

"What odds then! What odds, Mrs. Dilber?" said the woman. "Every person has a right to take care of themselves. He always did."

"That's true, indeed!" said the laundress. "No man more so."

*sepulchres — monuments

Starting with this extract, explore how Dickens presents the suffering of the poor in *A Christmas Carol*.

Write about:
- how Dickens presents the suffering of the poor in this extract
- how Dickens presents the suffering of the poor in the novel as a whole. [30]

Your answer may include:

AO1 — show understanding of the text
- *The pawn broker's shop is in an unpleasant part of London that is "foul" and "wretched". Dickens shows the reality of life in the slums. This may have been eye-opening for some readers who were not aware of the conditions that some people lived in.*
- *It's implied that the thieves regularly visit the pawn broker (they aren't "strangers") even though they have jobs as a "charwoman", "laundress" and "undertaker's man". This suggests that they are not paid enough, as they must pawn items to make ends meet.*
- *The unpleasant characterisation of the poor in this extract contrasts sharply with how the Cratchit family are presented elsewhere in the novella. The Cratchits are poor, but they are loving, hard-working and honest, and their home is warm and welcoming. Dickens uses the Cratchits to challenge negative stereotypes that were associated with the poor.*
- *Although both Martha and Bob Cratchit are employed, the family can only afford to rent a small house, their Christmas dinner is "Eked out" with cheap ingredients and they cook their goose at the bakers because they cannot afford fuel. Like the thieves, it's suggested that Bob and Martha are barely paid enough.*
- *In Stave One, Scrooge is unsympathetic towards the poor. He thinks that poor people should go to workhouses and prisons, and he doesn't want to donate to the charity collectors.*

AO2 — show understanding of the writer's language choices
- *Dickens uses a list of three ("with crime, with filth and misery") to emphasise the unpleasant nature of the area where the pawn shop is located.*
- *The adjective "slunk" suggests that the woman's movements are secretive and animalistic. This makes her seem sly and dehumanises her.*
- *Unpleasant imagery of "corrupted fat" and "sepulchres of bones". These negative descriptions have hellish connotations to convey just how awful the conditions are.*

AO3 — relate the novella to the context
- *Dickens implies that poverty leads to other societal issues such as crime, antisocial behaviour ("the people half-naked, drunken") and unsanitary conditions ("cesspools, disgorged their offences of smell, and dirt"). Dickens believed that ignoring the problem of poverty could lead to the "Doom" of mankind.*
- *Dickens was critical of the way the poor were treated. Society's answer to the issue of poverty was punishment in the form of prisons, the workhouse and the treadmill. Dickens argues that fairer wages and compassion were better solutions to the problem of poverty.*

This answer should be marked in accordance with the levels-based mark scheme on page 61.

Make sure your answer to this question is in paragraphs and full sentences. Bullet points have been used in this example answer to suggest some information you could include.

EXAMINATION PRACTICE

In this extract from Stave Four, the Ghost of Christmas Yet to Come takes Scrooge to a churchyard. The ghost shows Scrooge what his grave may look like in the future.

The Spirit stood among the graves, and pointed down to One. He advanced towards it trembling. The Phantom was exactly as it had been, but he dreaded that he saw new meaning in its solemn shape.

"Before I draw nearer to that stone to which you point," said Scrooge, "answer me one question. Are these the shadows of the things that Will be, or are they shadows of things that May be, only?"

Still the Ghost pointed downward to the grave by which it stood.

"Men's courses will foreshadow certain ends, to which, if persevered in, they must lead," said Scrooge. "But if the courses be departed from, the ends will change. Say it is thus with what you show me!"

The Spirit was immovable as ever.

Scrooge crept towards it, trembling as he went; and following the finger, read upon the stone of the neglected grave his own name, EBENEZER SCROOGE.

"Am I that man who lay upon the bed?" he cried, upon his knees.

The finger pointed from the grave to him, and back again.

"No, Spirit! Oh no, no!"

The finger still was there.

"Spirit!" he cried, tight clutching at its robe, "hear me! I am not the man I was. I will not be the man I must have been but for this intercourse. Why show me this, if I am past all hope!"

For the first time the hand appeared to shake.

"Good Spirit," he pursued, as down upon the ground he fell before it: "Your nature intercedes for me, and pities me. Assure me that I yet may change these shadows you have shown me, by an altered life!"

The kind hand trembled.

"I will honour Christmas in my heart, and try to keep it all the year. I will live in the Past, the Present, and the Future. The Spirits of all Three shall strive within me. I will not shut out the lessons that they teach. Oh, tell me I may sponge away the writing on this stone!"

In his agony, he caught the spectral hand. It sought to free itself, but he was strong in his entreaty, and detained it. The Spirit, stronger yet, repulsed him.

Holding up his hands in a last prayer to have his fate reversed, he saw an alteration in the Phantom's hood and dress. It shrunk, collapsed, and dwindled down into a bedpost.

Starting with this extract, explore how Dickens presents Scrooge's fears in *A Christmas Carol*.

Write about:

- how Dickens presents what Scrooge is frightened of in this extract
- how Dickens presents Scrooge's fears in the novel as a whole. [30]

LEVELS-BASED MARK SCHEMES FOR EXTENDED RESPONSE QUESTIONS

Questions that require extended writing use mark bands. The whole answer will be marked together to determine which mark band it fits into and which mark should be awarded within the mark band.

The descriptors have been written in simple language to give an indication of the expectations of each mark level. See the AQA website for the official mark schemes used.

Level	Students' answers tend to...
6 **(26–30 marks)**	• Focus on the text as conscious construct (i.e. a story written by Dickens intended to have a deliberate effect). • Produce a logical and well-structured response which closely uses the text to explore their argument / interpretation. • Analyse the writer's craft by considering the effects of a writer's choice, linked closely to meanings. • Understand the writer's purpose and context.
5 **(21–25 marks)**	• Start to think about ideas in a more developed way. • Think about the deeper meaning of a text and start to explore alternative interpretations. • Start to focus on specific elements of writer's craft, linked to meanings. • Focus more on abstract concepts, such as themes and ideas, than narrative events or character feelings.
4 **(16–20 marks)**	• Sustain a focus on an idea, or a particular technique. • Start to consider how the text works and what the writer is doing. • Use examples effectively to support their points. • Explain the effect of a writer's method on the text, with a clear focus on it having been consciously written. • Show an understanding of ideas and themes.
3 **(11–15 marks)**	• Explain their ideas. • Demonstrate knowledge of the text as a whole. • Show awareness of the concept of themes. • Identify the effects of a range of methods on reader.
2 **(6–10 marks)**	• Support their comments by using references to / from the text. • Make comments that are generally relevant to the question. • Identify at least one method and possibly make some comment on the effect of it on the reader.
1 **(1–5 marks)**	• Describe the text. • Retell the narrative. • Make references to, rather than use references from, the text.
0 marks	Nothing worthy of credit / nothing written.

EXAMINATION PRACTICE ANSWERS

Throughout the novella, Dickens uses fear as a motivator to encourage Scrooge to learn the error of his ways and set him on the path to redemption. This begins in Stave One with the appearance of Marley's ghost, and reaches a climax in this extract from Stave Four where the Ghost of Christmas Yet to Come shows Scrooge a version of the future where he has not redeemed himself. Although each of the ghosts elicit a variety of emotions from Scrooge, including happiness and sadness, it is arguably fear which has the most significant impact on Scrooge's desire to change.

In this extract, Scrooge is frightened that it is too late to redeem himself, and that the visions shown by the Ghost of Christmas Yet to Come will come true. Scrooge is fearful that people will not mourn his passing, and that his death will be quickly forgotten, as suggested by his *"neglected"* grave. Dickens shows Scrooge's fear as he approaches the grave with the use of the verb *"crept"*. This implies Scrooge's reluctance to look at the grave and face what he has probably suspected all along: that he is the dead man. Scrooge's fear is also emphasised with his use of exclamations, for example *"No, Spirit! Oh no, no!"*. This conveys Scrooge's strength of emotion and his desperation to change the course of his fate. Scrooge's fear is also emphasised by his use of imperative verbs, such as *"Say"*, *"hear"* and *"Assure"* as he begs the Ghost of Christmas Yet to Come. These command verbs highlight Scrooge's desperation and his urgency to be reassured by the ghost that he still has the opportunity to change. The cumulative effect of these techniques is to clearly convey Scrooge's fear and distress. Seeing a grown man display such raw emotions would have shocked Victorian readers, particularly because people were expected to suppress strong emotions and to behave in a polite and reserved manner.

Scrooge is visited by several ghosts, but he is most afraid of the Ghost of Christmas Yet to Come. The ghost is characterised as sinister and mysterious; it doesn't speak and the appearance is similar to that of the Grim Reaper, the personification of death. Dickens never describes the ghost's face to the reader, and he may have chosen to present the ghost in this way to represent how the future is unknown. Characterising the Ghost of Christmas Yet to Come as a frightening, death-like spectre reinforces the seriousness of the ghost's message about change and redemption. Using fear to reinforce a serious message is also seen in Stave One, where Marley's ghost is presented as frightening with *"death-cold eyes"*. Marley's ghost also has an important message to impart to Scrooge about the consequences of his selfish behaviour.

Dickens also hoped that the fear of punishment in the afterlife would also resonate with his readers. Since Dickens' Victorian readers were mainly Christians, they would have been very familiar with the ideas of heaven and hell. Marley warns Scrooge that if he continues to be greedy and selfish, he will be punished in the afterlife. This punishment is an eternal purgatory where spirits are unable to help those in the mortal world, as shown by the restless phantoms who cannot intervene in the world of the living. Dickens wanted readers of *A Christmas Carol* to realise that they needed to act with more compassion towards those who were less fortunate, especially those living in poverty. Dickens hoped that fear of this purgatory may have encouraged readers to act with more generosity and kindness.

INDEX

A
allegory 10, 25, 46
alliteration 11, 31
Assessment Objectives vi

B
Belle 20, 32

C
chain 17
charity collectors 5, 6, 8, 15, 16, 30, 49, 52, 56
child labour 5
Christianity 30, 40, 42, 47, 52
Christmas spirit 52, 53
class 4
  middle class 4, 8
  upper class 4, 8
  working class 3, 4, 5, 6, 23
comic relief 12
context 4–8
Cratchit, Belinda 40
Cratchit, Bob 5, 6, 14, 19, 23, 28, 30, 39, 49
Cratchit family 40, 53, 56
Cratchit, Martha 5, 40
Cratchit, Mrs 23, 24, 28, 40
Cratchit, Peter 40

D
Dickens, Charles 2, 8
Doom 25, 46
doorknocker 16
dramatic irony 10, 26, 33

E
exclamations 11, 25

F
Fan 18
Fezziwig 19, 53
foil 10, 14, 36
food 8
foreshadowing 10, 13, 14, 16, 32
Fred 14, 15, 18, 24, 28, 30, 36, 37, 49, 52

G
Ghost of Christmas Past 18–20, 28, 41, 48
Ghost of Christmas Present 16, 21–25, 42, 48, 53
Ghost of Christmas Yet to Come 4, 26–28, 43, 48
ghost story 2, 13
Grim Reaper 26, 43

H
housing 6
humbug 15
humour 12

I
Ignorance and Want 25, 46, 57
imperative verbs 18, 25
Industrial Revolution 6

J
Jesus 21, 42
juxtaposition 12

L
language techniques 10
London 4

M
Malthus, Thomas 8
Marley's ghost 17, 38, 47
Marley, Jacob 13, 38
metaphor 12, 17
morality tale 3

N
narrator 9, 14
novella 9
nutrition 6

O
Old Joe 27, 57
onomatopoeia 11

P
pace 19, 24, 25
personification 12
Poor Law 8
poverty 6, 7, 15, 25, 31, 46, 56
prisons 7
puns 12
purgatory 17

R
redemption 47–49
rhetorical questions 11

S
Sabbatarianism 22
scabbard 42
Scrooge, Ebeneezer 4–6, 13, 15–33, 47, 53, 56
sensory language 11
simile 12
slums 6, 27
Stave One 13– 17
Stave Two 18–20
Stave Three 21–25
Stave Four 26–28
Stave Five 29, 30
staves 9
structure 49
symbolism 10, 21, 31, 41

T
Three thieves 27, 57
time hops 2, 9
Tiny Tim 23, 28, 30, 40, 56
tone 29
torch 21, 22, 42
treadmill 7
turkey 29

V
Victorian era 3–8

W
workhouse 7, 8, 15

ACKNOWLEDGMENTS

The questions in the ClearRevise textbook are the sole responsibility of the authors and have neither been provided nor approved by the examination board.

Every effort has been made to trace and acknowledge ownership of copyright. The publishers will be happy to make any future amendments with copyright owners that it has not been possible to contact. The publisher would like to thank the following companies and individuals who granted permission for the use of their images in this textbook.

Page 2 — Charles Dickens © Everett Collection / Shutterstock

Page 3 — A Christmas Carol frontpiece © The History Collection / Alamy Stock Photo

Page 5 — An engraving depicting a London chimney sweep © World History Archive / Alamy Stock Photo

Page 6 — Liverpool: slum, c.1840 © GRANGER - Historical Picture Archive / Alamy Stock Photo

Page 7 — Thomas Hood (1799-1845) the separation of husbands and wives in workhouses 1832 © Pictorial Press Ltd / Alamy Stock Photo

Page 7 — Treadmill at Brixton prison, London © World History Archive / Alamy Stock Photo

Page 13 — © Donald Cooper / Photostage

Page 14 — © Donald Cooper / Photostage

Page 16 — The Ghostly Knocker © Classic Image / Alamy Stock Photo

Page 17 — © Donald Cooper / Photostage

Page 18 — © Donald Cooper / Photostage

Page 19 — Christmas Carol © Chronicle / Alamy Stock Photo

Page 20 — A Christmas Carol. Christmas at Belle's family © GRANGER - Historical Picture Archive / Alamy Stock Photo

Page 21 — © Donald Cooper / Photostage

Page 23 — © Donald Cooper / Photostage

Page 30 — A Christmas Carol. Scrooge arriving for Christmas dinner © GRANGER - Historical Picture Archive / Alamy Stock Photo

Page 31 — © Donald Cooper / Photostage

Page 32 — Charles Dickens's 'A Christmas Carol' © Lebrecht Music & Arts / Alamy Stock Photo

Page 33 — © Donald Cooper / Photostage

Page 36 — © Donald Cooper / Photostage

Page 38 — © Donald Cooper / Photostage

Page 39 — © Donald Cooper / Photostage

Page 40 — © Donald Cooper / Photostage

Page 41 — © Donald Cooper / Photostage

Page 42 — © Donald Cooper / Photostage

Page 43 — Tiny Tim from A Christmas Carol by Jessie Wilcox Smith © RTRO / Alamy Stock Photo

Page 46 — A Christmas Carol. Ignorance and Want. © GRANGER - Historical Picture Archive / Alamy Stock Photo

Page 47 — © Donald Cooper / Photostage

Page 48 — © Donald Cooper / Photostage

Page 49 — © Donald Cooper / Photostage

Page 53 — © Donald Cooper / Photostage

Page 56 — © Donald Cooper / Photostage

EXAMINATION TIPS

With your examination practice, use a boundary approximation using the following table. Be aware that the grade boundaries can vary from year to year, so they should be used as a guide only.

Grade	9	8	7	6	5	4	3	2	1
Boundary	88%	79%	71%	61%	52%	43%	31%	21%	10%

1. Read the question carefully. Don't give an answer to a question that you *think* is appearing (or wish was appearing!) rather than the actual question.

2. Spend time reading through the extract, and think about what happens before and after, and how it links to other parts of the novella. The statement above the extract will help you identify where in the novella it is from.

3. It's worth jotting down a quick plan to make sure your answer includes sufficient detail and is focused on the question.

4. The question will ask you about the extract and the novella as a whole, but you don't need to spend an equal amount of time on both. If you're struggling to make close textual references about the extract, you can concentrate on the rest of the novella instead.

5. Start your answer with a brief introduction where you summarise the main points of your response. This can help your answer to stay on-track.

6. A discussion of Dickens' methods can include his language choices, but also structural choices (such as the ordering of events), how characters develop, and what their actions tell you about their characterisation.

7. Include details from the text to support your answer. These details might be quotes, or they can be references to the text.

8. Make sure your handwriting is legible. The examiner can't award you marks if they can't read what you've written.

9. The examiner will be impressed if you can correctly use technical terms like 'dramatic irony', 'metaphor', 'allegory', 'personification' etc, but to get the best marks you need to explore the effect of these techniques.

10. Use linking words and phrases to show you are developing your points or comparing information, for example, "this reinforces", "this shows that" and "on the other hand". This helps to give your answer structure, and makes it easier for the examiner to award you marks.

11. If you need extra paper, make sure you clearly signal that your answer is continued elsewhere. Remember that longer answers don't necessarily score more highly than shorter, more concise answers.

Good luck!

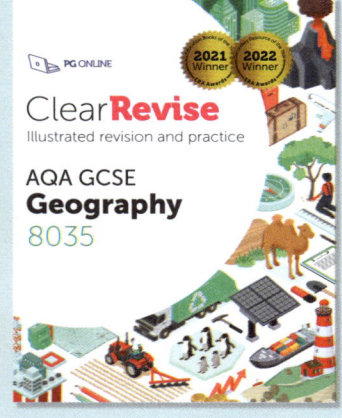